pocket dictionary
of
Irish Myth & legend

Ronan Coghlan

An Appletree Pocket Book

appletree press

Published and printed by
The Appletree Press Ltd
7 James Street South
Belfast BT2 8DL
1985

9 8 7 6 5 4 3

© Appletree Press Ltd, 1985

Illustrated by Bridget Murray

British Library Cataloguing in Publication Data
Coghlan, Ronan
Pocket dictionary of Irish myth and legend.
1. Mythology, Irish—Dictionaries
2. Legends—Ireland—Dictionaries
I. Title
299'.162'0321   BL980.17

ISBN 0-86281-152-X

CONTENTS

Note on Pronunciation   4

Introduction   5

Dictionary of Irish Myth and Legend   7

Bibliography   71

note on pronunciation

The pronunciation of the Irish names in this dictionary poses a problem as many of the names are in early Irish forms. The following is a rough guide to modern Irish pronunciation and may prove of some assistance to the reader.

Letters have the same phonetic values as in English, except for the following:

a is pronounced like *o* in cot or *aw* in thaw
bh is pronounced like *v* or *w*
ch is pronounced like *ch* in Bach
c is pronounced like *k*, never like *s*
dh is pronounced like *y* or is unpronounced
fh is unpronounced
gh is pronounced like *y* or is unpronounced
mh is pronounced like *v* or *w*
s is pronounced like *sh* when it precedes i or e
sh is pronounced like *h*
th is pronounced like *h*

introduction

It must be stated at the outset that this volume is not another retelling of the myths of Ireland. Such retellings exist in profusion. Rather it is a handy reference work — if you will, a who's who, what's what and where's where of the vast corpus of Irish myth. It does not pretend to do justice to the poetry of that myth.

What, we must ask, is meant by the terms 'myth' and 'legend' and just what territory is this work designed to cover? By myths we mean tales of the gods, relating to such events as the creation, the relationship of one god to another, their battles with giants, demons and other such adversaries, and how they were responsible for such things as the formation of natural landmarks. By legends we denote tales about historical or supposedly historical persons, places, objects or events, these often containing a supernatural element.

Our knowledge of Irish mythology comes from mediaeval documents. When these were written, the Irish had become Christians and no longer worshipped the ancient gods. However, these had not been forgotten: they had merely been demoted to the status of a prehistoric race, the Tuatha De Danaan, whose humanity was, in fact, but a thin veneer. For example, one of their leaders was the Dagda, whose very name means 'the good god'. The mediaeval Irish believed in other prehistoric races too and to these beliefs they added elements which had their roots in the Bible, the Apocrypha and the classics.

Mediaeval Ireland had as its dominant race the Gaelic or Goidelic Celts, of which the Gaelic Scots were an offshoot. The Gaels believed they had taken over the island from the Tuatha De Danaan and a large body of legend is set in the Gaelic period. This falls into three cycles:

(a) the Ulster Cycle, which tells of the deeds of the Red Branch and particularly its chief hero, Cuchulain;
(b) the Finn Cycle, dealing with the exploits of Finn mac Cool and the Fianna; and
(c) the Cycles of the Kings, dealing with such persons as Conn of the Hundred Battles and Cormac mac Art.

Just where legend ends and history begins in these is difficult to determine. The Finn Cycle seems to be entirely myth, but there may be elements of genuine history in the other two.

Irish myths are paralleled by those of the ancient Britons

whose gods, euhemerised in the same way as the Irish ones, are to be found in the traditions of the mediaeval Welsh. The Continental Celts had similar beliefs, so far as we can judge from the scant references to be found in classical literature and the information to be derived from archaeological investigation. Thus, the Irish had a god Lugh, equating to the British Lleu and the Continental Lugos.

Hitherto, while poetic renditions of Irish myths have been available in plenty, no comprehensive handbook such as the present work has been on the market. It is hoped it will assist the reader who wants to check quickly who an Irish god was or what an Irish hero did. The present writer hopes it will fill a gap which has existed for some time.

dictionary of Irish Myth & legend

Abarta, the name of the Giolla Deacar.

Abhean, the harper of the Tuatha De Danaan, who was brought to them from the hills by the Men of the Three Gods.

Accasbel, a Partholonian who built the first inn in Ireland.

Adhnuall, a hound of Finn, once stolen by Arthur, son of the king of Britain. He strayed after a battle in Leinster and made a circuit of Ireland three times. He returned to the battlefield, came to a hill where three Fenians and their lovers were buried, gave three howls and died.

Adna, a legendary early explorer in Ireland, sent by King Ninus of Assyria.

Aedan, a warrior who slew Mael Fhothartaig, son of Ronan, king of Leinster, at the king's behest. He was himself slain by the victim's sons.

Aedh. 1. The father of Macha the Red.

2. A legendary king of Oriel who carried a shield which usually had one of the badba perched on its rim. It was called *Dubhghiolla,* 'black servant'.

3. The dwarf of Fergus mac Leide, who accompanied Eisirt to the leprechaun kingdom of Iubdan.

4. A son of Finn.

5. The original name of Goll.

6. The son of Ainmire and king of Tara who made war on Branduff, king of Leinster. He was defeated and, as he had left behind the cowl given him by Saint Columba, which protected him from being slain, he perished at the hand of Branduff or that of his spy, Ron Cerr. One may compare the power of Aedh's cowl to that of King Arthur's scabbard.

7. Son of Bodb Dearg.

8. Son of Lir.

Aengus. 1. The Irish love-god, son of the Dagda, he was of beauteous appearance and was accompanied by birds.

2. Aengus Bolg was the ancestor of the Firbolg and was later regarded as the ancestor of the Deisi, an early Irish tribe.

3. A member of the Deisi who slew Ceallach and injured his father, Cormac mac Art. This led to the expulsion of the Deisi to the Decies in Waterford.

4. Son of Bodb Dearg.

Agnoman, the father of Nemed.

Ai, the poet of the Tuatha De Danaan. When his mother was expecting him, the house was shaken by a wind. A druid foretold that the child within his mother's womb would be a marvel.

Aibell, a fairy queen of North Munster who had an especial connection with the O'Briens.

Aichleach, the slayer of Finn, according to one legend.

Aige, a daughter of Broccaid mac Bric, she was, through envy, turned into a fawn and slain by the warriors of Meilge, the high king.

Ailell, the husband of Maeve and king of Connacht.

Aimend, according to mediaeval legend she was a daughter of the king of Corco Loigde. In fact, she was a sun goddess manifestation.

Aine, a notable fairy queen, perhaps a daughter of Manannan, perhaps identical with the Morrigan, perhaps identical with Anu. Her dwelling place is Knockainy, which is in Irish *Cnoc Aine,* 'Aine's Hill'. Wisps of straw used to be set alight in her honour on Saint John's Eve, hence her name Aine of the Wisps *(na gCliar)*. She is invoked against sickness. The plant meadow-sweet is associated with her. In ancient legend she was raped by the king of Munster. She was the mother of Earl Gerald.

Ainnle, a son of Usnach and brother of Naoise.

Airioch Feabhruadh, a son of Milesius, born to Seang.

Airmed, the sister of Miach, she laid out on her cloak, according to their virtue, the herbs which had grown on his grave; but Diancecht mixed them up, so that their virtue remains unknown.

Aitheach-Tuatha, pre-Gaelic people of Ireland who staged a revolt against the Milesians. This was successful, but eventually power fell once more into Milesian hands.

Aithechda, the son of Magog who was the ancestor of all invaders of Ireland after the Deluge.

Amairgene, the father of Conall Cearnach and slayer of the Three-Headed Bird.

Amazons, in Greek legend, races of warrior women in Asia and Africa. The tale of the Asiatic Amazons may have been based on traditions of the beardless Hittites. In Irish legend, they were said to be descended from

Iobath, son of Magog. The descendants of Gael had to pass through their territory.

Amergin. 1. A Milesian invader, one of Milesius's sons.

2. A warrior of Fergus mac Leide.

Andoid, one of the four outside the Ark, who, in Irish legend, survived the Deluge.

Anind, a son of Nemed. When he died and his grave was being dug, Loch Ennell burst forth.

Anluan, a Connacht warrior slain by Conall Cearnach. He was the brother of Cet.

Anu, an important goddess of the pagan Irish, the mother of the gods and the goddess of prosperity. The Paps of Anu (Dana) in County Kerry were named after her. She was to some degree confused with Dana.

Aobh, the wife of Lir, mother by him of Fionnuala, Aedh, Fiachra and Conn.

Aiobhell, a fairy woman who lived at Craig Liath (the Grey Rock), the lover of Dubhlaing ua Artigan and possessor of a magic harp. Whosoever heard its music would not live long thereafter.

Aoibinn, alternative name for Aibell.

Aoife. 1. A warrior woman who made war on Scathach when Cuchulain was training with her. Cuchulain defeated her

Aoife, the warrior woman

in battle but spared her life. She became his lover and bore him a son.

2. The second wife of Lir, who changed his children into swans. As a punishment, she was changed into a witch of the air.

3. The lover of Ilbrec, son of Manannan, she was transformed into a crane. Her skin was used to make the Treasure Bag of the Fianna.

Aonbharr, a legendary horse which could travel on both land and sea.

Aoncos, an island supported by a single pillar seen by Maeldun on his voyage.

Arannan, a son of Milesius, born in Galicia.

Ardan, a son of Usnach and brother of Naoise.

Art, legendary high king. On his way to engage Lugaid mac Con, a rebel king, in battle he passed the night at the dwelling of the smith, Olc Aiche, and, by his daughter, Achtan, became the father of Cormac. Knowing his death had been prophesied, he gave her his sword, his golden ring and his ceremonial clothing.

Arthur, a son of the king of Britain who stole three of Finn's hounds, Bran, Sceolan and Adhnuall. He was pursued to Britain by a party of Fianna, who recovered the hounds. Arthur made a bond with Finn to be his follower.

Artrach, son of Bodb Dearg.

Artur, a son of Nemed, born in Ireland, who led the Nemedians in a disastrous battle against the Fomorians at Cramh Ros.

Ath Liag Finn, the name of the ford into which Finn dropped a flat stone with a golden chain attached to it, a present brought by a daughter of Mongan of the Sidhe. The stone will be found and brought to land by the Woman of the Waves on a Sunday morning, seven years before the end of the world.

Babal, a Partholonian who introduced cattle into Ireland.

Bachorbladhra, a Partholonian, the first foster-father in Ireland.

Badb, a war goddess. Sometimes regarded as the same as Nemain, she may have been an aspect of the Morrigan. Her name means 'crow' and she could appear in that guise. She was the wife of Net.

Badba, supernatural creatures who frequented battlefields.

Badh, a name given to the banshee in East Munster.

Bainleannan, a female spirit.

Balba, a companion of Cesair on her voyage.

Balor, a leader of the Fomorians with an evil eye which could destroy whoever gazed on it. It was prophesied that his grandson would kill him, so when, despite precautions, his daughter Ethlinn gave birth he had her child, Lugh, cast into the sea. However, he was saved and later slew Balor in a battle between the Fomorians and the Tuatha De Danaan.

Banba, one of the three women who met the Tuatha De Danaan when they landed and asked that they call the island after her, which they did. According to another legend, she was a daughter of Cain who lived in Ireland before the Flood and gave her name to it. She was originally a goddess.

Banshee, a female fairy attached to a family who warns it of an approaching death by giving an eerie wail. The banshee is found both in Scottish and Irish lore. The word means 'woman of the Sidhe'.

Barinthus, the personage who told Saint Brendan about the Land Promised to the Saints.

Barran, a companion of Cesair on her voyage.

Beag, this member of the Tuatha de Danaan had a magic well guarded by his three daughters. Once Finn came towards the well and the three wished to prevent his approach. One threw well water over him and some of it went into his mouth and from that he gained wisdom.

Beara, a daughter of the king of Spain, it was once prophesied to her that her husband would arrive that night and she was told to go to the River Eibhear, perhaps the Ebro, where she would find a salmon wearing shining clothing.

Bebind, a divine being, the mother of Fraoch and a sister of Boann.

Bebo, the queen to Iubdan, who accompanied him to Emhain Macha.

Becfola, the wife to Dermot, king of Tara. She fell in love with Flann and eventually eloped with him.

Beltane, the festival of the beginning of the summer of the Celtic year, falling on 1 May. It was customary to celebrate this festival with bonfires.

Beothach, the son of Iarbanel.

Bile, this word denotes 'a sacred tree' in Irish.

Biobal, a Partholonian who introduced gold into Ireland.

Birog, a druidess who aided Cian to penetrate Balor's tower and who later saved the life of Lugh when he fell into the water.

Bith. 1. The son of Noah and father of Cesair.
2. The father of Adna.

Black Pig, a boar with magic properties which was chased through Ulster and then into Connacht, where it was killed in the Valley of the Black Pig in County Sligo. A mound marks its grave.

Blathnad, the wife of Cu Roi, who was carried off by her husband from Scotland. She assisted Cuchulain to murder him, but Fercherdne, his poet, avenged him. Noticing Blathnad standing on the verge of a cliff, he caught her round the waist and jumped over the edge, killing them both.

Bo, the name of a destructive species of fairy, perhaps of Scottish origin, found in the marshes of County Down.

Boann, a water goddess, wife of Nechtan and mother, by the Dagda, of Aengus; associated with the River Boyne. When she said a well was powerless waves from it broke on her and took off a thigh, a hand and an eye. Boann fled to the mouth of the Boyne where she was drowned. The name 'Boann' may signify 'cow white goddess'.

Bochra, the father of Fintan. His name signifies 'ocean'.

Bodb Dearg, one of the Tuatha De Danaan, a son of the Dagda, he ruled Connacht.

Bran. 1. The son of Febal. One day he heard music behind him which lulled him to sleep. When he awoke he found a silver branch beside him. When he returned home he saw the woman who had played the music. She told him she had brought the branch from a marvellous country. She disappeared and Bran set off to find her land. On his voyage he saw Manannan driving his chariot over the waves. To him they were a plain and the salmon were calves or lambs. They came to a Land of Joy which one refused to leave. Then they came to Tir na mBan of which the mysterious woman was ruler. There they stayed for many years, but thought only a single year had passed. They then said they wished to return, but the queen said they would regret it. On coming back to Ireland the inhabitants told them that Bran had set out in olden times. One of Bran's followers jumped ashore and was reduced to ashes. Bran set off once more on his ship.

Bran is generally thought to have been a Celtic god, reduced to human stature. There was also a British Bran, called Bendegeidfran (blest Bran) in the Mabinogion, where he is depicted as a giant who led an attack on Ireland. This would be an indication that the god Bran was revered on both sides of the Irish Sea. His name signifies 'raven'.

2. The hound of Finn mac Cool and also his nephew, for Finn's sister, Tuirean, was turned into a bitch, in which state she gave birth to Bran and Sceolan. Once Bran was chasing a fawn. The fawn spoke to Finn and Finn told it to run through his legs, which it did. Bran pursued it and, to save the fawn, Finn crushed the hound with his legs. It was said that the fawn was Ossian's mother. It was also said the fawn was Finn's mother, under enchantment.

Brandan, a variant and less preferable form of Brendan.

Jasconius, the whale encountered by Brendan on his voyage

Branduff, a king of Leinster who died, according to the Annals of Ulster, in 604. His father was Eochu, king of Leinster, and his mother's name was Feidelm. She gave birth to twin sons and exchanged one for one of the twin daughters of Aidan, king of Scotland. The other, Branduff, became king of Leinster. He tricked Mongan into giving him his wife, though Mongan later tricked him into returning her. By treachery he tried to kill the son of the high king Aedh and, although the latter escaped, he was slain before he reached home. Aedh made war on Branduff, but the latter smuggled men into Aedh's camp and defeated him. Branduff was killed by Saran. According to legend, he was raised from the dead by a miracle.

Breg, the name of a wife of the Dagda, also called Meng and Meabal. These may all be titles rather than names and may have been applied to Boann.

Brendan, an historical saint whose legendary voyage is recounted in the *Navigatio Sancti Brendani*. Brendan was told by Barinthus of the Land Promised to the Saints and set sail for there. The following are the features of the voyage: (i) an island where the travellers sheltered in a large building; (ii) an island of sheep; (iii) the whale Jasconius, which was mistaken for an island; (iv) an island of spirits in bird form; (v) the Island of Saint Ailbe; (vi) a curdled sea, possibly the Sargasso; (vii) a large island; (viii) the Island of Strong Men which had three classes of inhabitants — boys, young men and elders — and contained purple fruit called scaltae; (ix) an island of grape trees; (x) an area of clear water, where they could gaze down to the bottom; (xi) a crystal column, perhaps an iceberg; (xii) an island of gigantic smiths; (xiii) a smoking and flaming mountain; (xiv) a man-shaped cloud on a rock mass which was Judas let off damnation on Sundays; (xv) the island of Paul the Hermit; and (xvi) the Land Promised to the Saints.

Some of these places were visited more than once. After they reached the Land Promised to the Saints, they travelled for forty days. They came to a broad, deep, impassable river. Here a young man told Brendan to turn back, that the land would be revealed to his Christian successors in troubled times. According to the life of the saint there were two journeys. The first, in a curragh, was unsuccessful, so Brendan returned to Ireland and set off again in a wooden ship.

Breoga, a Partholonian who introduced monomachy into Ireland.

Bres, a beautiful half-Fomorian who was made king of the Tuatha De Danaan when Nuada became incapacitated. An unpopular ruler, when Nuada again became eligible to reign he was deposed and sought his Fomorian father to get aid for vengeance. Captured at the Battle of Moytura, he promised the Tuatha agricultural favours and gave them advice about ploughing and sowing and so his life was spared.

Bresal, the high king of the world who built the wooden fortress, Barc Bresail, in Leinster. It was destroyed in the reign of King Eochu by the Ulstermen, who were supporting Tuathal Techtmar.

Bri, the daughter of Midir. Leith was her unsuccessful suitor.

Brian, one of the sons of Tuireann.

Bricriu, a personage of the Ulster Cycle, known for his bitter tongue and his desire to stir up trouble.

Brigid, an early goddess whose name signifies 'the high one'. She would appear to have been a counterpart of Brigantia, the goddess of the Brythonic Brigantes. She would seem to have been a triune goddess, as she was said to have two sisters, also called Brigid. She was a daughter of the Dagda. The saint of the name is usually regarded as an historical personage to whom legends of the goddess have attached themselves. Giraldus Cambrensis speaks of her perpetual fire. This was enclosed by a hedge and could not be approached by males. This has been seen as a relic of Brigid worship.

According to a theory put forward by R. A. S. Mac-Alister, Brigid the saint was originally a priestess of Brigid the goddess, converted to Christianity. The head of a community of Brigid priestesses, she transformed this into a community of nuns.

Britan, one of the Nemedians who, having fled to Ireland when the Formorians overcame that race, settled with his family in Britain to which island his name was given.

Bui, a name applied to the Cailleach Beara. As 'Cailleach Beara' is a title, this may have been her personal name.

Buinne, a son of Fergus mac Roi. When the sons of Usnach were attacked at the House of the Red Branch, he and his brother Iollan were supposed to be defending them. Buinne slew many of Conor's men and then Conor offered him a mountain as a reward if he would cease fighting, which he accepted. Thereafter the mountain turned barren.

Cael, the suitor of Credhe, who won her by reciting a poem in praise of her possessions. He went to woo her in company with the Fianna.

Cahir More, a legendary high king killed by Conn of the Hundred Battles who succeeded him.

Cailleach Beara, called in English 'the Hag of Beare', she was an important figure in Irish legend — probably a goddess; perhaps, with her sisters, the Witches of Bolus and Dingle, originally a triune goddess. She figures largely in Irish and Scottish folklore. According to one work dealing with Scottish folklore her name really means 'the Blue Hag'. She had seven youthful periods during which she married seven different husbands, who each grew old and died. According to the Book of Lecan she was associated with Beare because she had fifty foster-children there. She was the queen of the Limerick fairies. She dropped the cairns on the hills of Meath from her apron. She moved islands and built mountains. She was also known as Bui and, when called by this name, she was regarded as the wife of Lugh. According to mediaeval legend, she eventually became a nun.

Cain, in the Bible, the son of Adam and Eve. According to legend, three of his daughters, together with his brother Seth, were the first to see Ireland.

Cairbre, when the Aitheach-Tuatha had overthrown the Milesians they set Cairbre Cathead over them to rule. He was so called because he had the ears of a cat.

Cairell, a son of Finn, killed by Goll.

Cairenn Chasdub, the mother of Niall of the Nine Hostages and apparently the secondary wife of Eochu Muigmedon. She was the daughter of Scal the Dumb, king of the Saxons. She was hated by Eochu's queen, Mongfhinn, and was forced to draw water from the well, even in late pregnancy. On one such excursion she gave birth to Niall.

Caladbolg, the magic sword of Cuchulain, thought to be the original of King Arthur's legendary sword Excalibur.

Camel, a doorkeeper at Tara in the reign of Nuada.

Cano, the story of this certainly historical character would seem to have been a definite element in the origin of the legend of Tristan (or Tristram), the lover of Iseult. He was a son of the king of Scotland in exile in Ireland and Marcan extended hospitality to him. Marcan was an old man and his wife Cred fell in love with Cano. She drugged all present at a feast and then endeavoured to seduce the object of her desires, but he said he could not accede to her request while an exile. However, he gave her a stone which contained his life. After his return to Scotland his designs to meet Cred were always frustrated by her stepson, Colcu. After one such frustration at Lough Crede she dashed her head on a rock and dropped the stone, which was thereby fragmented. Cano died three days later.

Caoilte, a member of the Fianna, said to have survived until the time of Saint Patrick. He was a nephew or cousin of Finn and a swift runner, speediest of all the Fianna.

Caoranach, a name given to the Lough Derg Monster.

Capa, one of the three fishermen whom legend makes the first discoverers of Ireland. They were driven there from Spain and decided to settle, but were destroyed by the Deluge.

Carman, this female came to Ireland from Athens. With her three ferocious sons — Valiant, Black and Evil, sons of Extinction and Darkness — she laid Ireland waste, but they were overcome by the Tuatha De Danaan. The sons were made depart and Carman died. The people of Leinster kept a festival in her honour. Carman was originally a goddess, a fact reinforced by the abstractions in her sons' pedigree.

Cassmail, one of the Tuatha De Danaan, slain at the Second Battle of Moytura.

Cat, in Irish lore black cats are lucky and the blood of a black cat is the cure to Saint Anthony's Fire (Erysipelas). Cats are said to understand human speech.

Cathal Crobhdhearg, a mediaeval king of Connacht, the brother of Rory O'Conor, last high king of Ireland. Cathal was illegitimate and the queen, hearing her husband the king of Connacht was to become a father, invoked the aid of a witch to prevent the birth. She hung up in her room a bundle of elder rods, tied with a magic string, knotted with nine knots, to bewitch the mother-to-be. However, the midwife frustrated the scheme.

Cathbad, a druid of Conor mac Nessa. He caused Cuchulain to take up arms by being overheard to say whosoever would take up arms on that day would be a glorious warrior, albeit a short-lived one. He also prophesied that Deirdre would be a great beauty and it was he who lured the sons of Usnach out of the Red Branch by sorcery. He also cursed Emhain Macha and Conor, because of Conor's slaying of them.

Ce, the druid of Nuada, mortally wounded in the Second Battle of Moytura. A lake, Lough Ce, burst over his grave.

Cellach, a son of Cormac mac Art, slain by the Deisi tribesman Aengus.

Celtchair, a legendary Ulster warrior, famous for his prowess.

Cerbnad, a daughter-in-law of Partholon.

Cesair, the daughter of Bith and granddaughter of Noah. When Bith was denied a place in the Ark by Noah, Cesair advised him, Fintan and Ladra to build an idol, which they did. The idol advised them to build a ship and take refuge in it, but it could not tell them when the Flood would occur. They acted on the idol's counsel and were sailing for more than seven years before landing in Ireland. There, in due course, Bith died and Fintan, who had married Cesair, abandoned her before the Flood.

Cet, a Connacht warrior who delighted in slaying Ulstermen.

Cethlenn, the wife of Balor who fought in the Second Battle of Moytura and wounded the Dagda.

Cetshamhain, alternative name for Beltane.

Changeling, the idea that the fairies will steal a baby and leave one of their own folk, usually of a hideous aspect or wretched nature, in its place is widespread in Europe. Baptism is generally believed to be efficacious in preventing such designs. It need not be supposed the changeling itself is always in favour of these steps. In one Irish tale the changeling leads its foster-parent to the fairy queen that she may recover her child. In 1884 two women were arrested in Clonmel. Harbouring the belief that a neighbouring child was a changeling, they put it, naked, on a hot shovel to break the charm.

Cheiromancy, this does not seem to have been greatly employed in early Ireland, but it was not unknown. Conall Corc, king of Munster, was said to have had his palm read when a baby.

Ciabhan, the mortal lover of Cliona who brought her to Ireland.

Cian, one of the Tuatha De Danaan who, disguised as a woman, went to Balor's tower to retrieve his wonderful stolen cow, the Glas Gaibhnenn. Aided by the druidess Birog, he was able to speak with Ethlinn, daughter of Balor, of whom he became enamoured. He begat a son, Lugh, on her. According to one legend, he returned to Ireland and was slain by the sons of Tuireann. According to another, Balor killed him.

The belief that fairies would steal a baby and leave a 'changeling', one of their own, in its place was widespread throughout Europe.

Cical, a legendary early invader of Ireland. According to the Book of Invasions he preceded Parthalon; according to the *Annals of the Four Masters* he came after him.

Cical and his followers, who are described as Fomorians, lived by fishing and hunting birds. They offered resistance to Partholon when he landed. A battle took place at Magh Ibha and Cical was slain.

Cliona, an Irish goddess of great beauty. She had three colourful birds, sweet of song, which could lull the sick to sleep. They fed on the apples of the otherworld tree. She was later said to be the queen of the South Munster fairies, with a palace in Carraig Cliona, a large rock near Mallow. She was also said to have been a foreigner, drowned in Glendore Harbour. The sea makes for her a noise of lamentation called 'Cliona's Wave'.

Cloch Labhrais, an oracular stone in the south of Ireland. On one occasion a man, suspecting his wife of adultery, placed her on the stone and asked her to swear that his suspicions were unfounded. Seeing her lover on the horizon, she said she had no more sinned with anyone than she had with him on the horizon. Because she had told the truth, but in such a manner her husband misunderstood, the stone split.

Clock of Hell, according to the tinkers, is a clock in Hell that ticks for ever.

Clonnach, the brother of Teideach.

Cluricaune, a diminutive being in folklore, somewhat fond of alcohol. He may, in fact, be a leprechaun who has cast off his sobriety, though he may also constitute a distinct species.

Cnu, the dwarf of Finn.

Cobthach, the brother of Laoghaire Lorc, king of Ireland. By pretending to be dead, Cobthach slew his unsuspecting brother and he poisoned Ailell, Laoghaire's son, who was king of Leinster. Ailell's son, Maen, called Labraid, killed Cobthach.

Cohuleen Druith, a magical cap which enables merfolk, and others, to survive under the sea.

Coinn Iotair, the hound of rage, a dog belonging to Cromm Dubh.

Coirbre, the poet of Tuatha De Danaan who cursed Bres and forced him to resign.

Colcu, the stepson of Cred who frustrated her designs to meet with Cano for amorous dalliance.

Colum Cuaillemech, the smith of the Tuatha De Danaan.

Conaing, a leader of the Fomorians who resided on Tory Island and who levied tribute on the Nemedians who, in retaliation, attacked Tory and killed Conaing.

Conaire, legendary king of Tara, the son of Mess Buachalla, begotten on her by a mysterious Bird King the night before she married the then king, Eterscelae. She raised Conaire in secret, not telling him he was the supposed son of the high king and consequently a claimant to the kingship. In due course Eterscelae died. Conaire one day followed a flock of birds, stripping to pursue them through the sea. They turned into men and their leader identified himself as Conaire's father, telling him to go to Tara. Here he was expected, because he had been seen in the tarbhfheis. He was made king.

Conall, alternative name for Conlai.

Conall Cearnach, a warrior of Ulster, the slayer of Anluan. He may have been an euhemerised horned god.

Conan, one of the Fianna, who was regarded as something of a buffoon. The epithet *maol*, 'bald' was applied to him.

Conaran, a member of the Tuatha De Danaan, he had three daughters, hags, who captured Finn and certain of his followers. They were rescued by Goll, who slew two of the hags, whereupon the third released the prisoners.

Congal, a foster brother of Mael Fhothartaig. When the latter's stepmother's maid came to solicit his attentions, he was playing with Congal and Donn. He went away and Congal, noticing the girl's embarrassment, inquired as to what the matter was. When she told him, he told her in no wise to apprise Mael Fhothartaig of her mission, but that he, if she desired, would speak with Mael Fhothartaig on her behalf.

Conlai, a son of Cuchulain by Aoife. When Conlai was grown his mother sent him from Scotland to Ireland. He first defeated Conall Cearnach. Then Cuchulain, despite a warning from Emer that this foreigner could be none other than his son, fought with Conlai and mortally wounded him, whereupon Conlai revealed his identity to his father.

Conn, a son of Lir.

Conn of the Hundred Battles, a legendary prehistoric king of Ireland. One day his followers and he were enshrouded by mist and a man appeared casting missiles at them. On being warned that one of them was the king, he invited them to his house. There Conn met the Sovranty of Ireland, a girl seated on a crystalline chair, wearing a golden crown. Lugh was there also and he prophesied concerning Conn's descendants who would reign over Ireland.

Conor, the son of Ness. His father was said to have been either the druid Cathbad or Fachtna Fathach, king of Ulster. He was born at the same time as Christ in Palestine. Due to the devious behaviour of his mother, Fergus mac Roi, king of Ulster, was ousted from the kingship and Conor placed there in his stead. Conor was the uncle of Cuchulain and was king of Ulster at the time of that hero's exploits. He does not present a very edifying picture in his treatment of the sons of Usnach.

Cormac. 1. Cormac mac Art was a legendary high king whose reign may have occurred in the third century; though whether he was an historical character or a purely mythical personage cannot be satisfactorily determined. He was looked on with great reverence and it was said that the exploits of Finn mac Cool occurred in his time. He is also credited with causing the first water-mill to be constructed in Ireland. He succeeded to the throne by defeating his predecessor, Fergus the Black-toothed.

2. Cormac Conloingeas was the son of Conor mac Nessa. After his father's treachery towards the sons of Usnach, he assisted Fergus mac Roi in his attack on him. He then went to Connacht. When Conor was dying, he summoned Cormac home to become king. Cormac was warned on his way by a girl that death awaited him. He stopped overnight at a house and during the night was attacked by Connachtmen. Cormac could not resist, for Craiftine the harper, who lived nearby, lulled him and made him drowsy with his music and so Cormac was slain.

Corpre, a Tuatha De Danaan poet, who satirised Bres. This satire was the first in Ireland.

Country of Snow, a place from which men came to fight against the Fianna in the Battle of Gabhra.

Country of the Lion, a place from which men came to fight against the Fianna in the Battle of Gabhra.

Craiftine, a harper. His wife Sceanb was the lover of Cormac Conloingeas. In revenge, when Cormac was being attacked, Craiftine played his harp and rendered him slumbrous, so that he was slain. It was his harp which revealed the secret of the equine ears of Labraid Loingseach.

Cred, the wife of Marcan and the would-be-lover of Cano.

Credhe, the daughter of the king of Ciarraighe Luachra, she was won by Cael. She raised a great lament over the death of her husband and then gave up the ghost herself. They were buried together in a single grave.

Credne Cerd, the brassworker of the Tuatha De Danaan.

Creidne, a female warrior of the Fianna, who fought on both land and sea. She joined the Fianna because she had fled her home after an incestuous intrigue with her father which had resulted in three sons.

Crevan, a legendary high king who, accompanied by a bainleannan, led an expedition from which he brought back remarkable treasure.

Croagh Patrick, a mountain in the west of Ireland. Here Saint Patrick summoned the serpents and demons of Ireland and banished them into the sea.

Cromlech, according to Irish folk-belief, was an artificial stone circle which could cure barrenness.

Cuchulain, the greatest of the heroes of Irish legend

Cromm Cruach, the name of an early Irish idol, said to
have been the chief idol of the pagan Irish. The god
Cromm Cruach had a dozen under-gods. Human
sacrifice, it was said, was offered to him.

Cromm Dubh, an early Irish idol revered by the people of
Munster and Connacht. The first Sunday of August was
called Cromm Dubh's Sunday.

Cruacha, the maidservant of Etain who accompanied her
when she departed with Midir. Cruachan in Connacht
was named after her.

Crunnchu, the husband of Macha.

Cuchulain, the greatest of the heroes of Irish legend,
perhaps entirely mythical, an Irish version of the god
Esus worshipped by the Continental Celts. His real
name, Setanta, would connect him with the Setantii, a
British tribe. The son of the god Lugh or of Sualtim, the
husband of his mother, Dechtire, he obtained his name
by offering to replace the hound of Culan, which he had
killed. (In Irish *cú Chulain* — Cuchulain — signifies
'Culan's hound'). He took up arms on a day he
understood to be auspicious for one who aspired to be

a hero, although to take up arms on the day in question would also lead to a short life. He slew the three sons of Nechta Scene and on his way back from so doing, while mad with a sort of battle frenzy reminiscent of those of the berserkers, he tethered swans which flew over his chariot and made a stag run behind it. In addition, it was decorated with the heads of his foes. Mugain, queen of Ulster, led her women forth, unclothed, towards him. The hero was suffused with embarrassment and turned his head away, whereupon he was seized and immersed in three tubs of ice-cold water. The first of these burst, in the second the water boiled, but in the third it just grew warm.

Cuchulain is chiefly famed for his defence of Ulster from the Connachtmen when they sought the Brown Bull of Cuailgne. The Red Branch knights were in an enchanted sleep, but Cuchulain held the armies of Maeve at bay, engaging Connacht champions each day in single combat. At length he grew so weak that he had to lash himself to a post. The Connachtmen knew he was dead when a raven perched on his shoulder and an otter lapped his blood. The Ulstermen, awakened, then came to defend their territory.

Cuchulain's other adventures included his sojourn with Scathach; his saving of Dervorgill; his being chosen champion of Ireland by Cu Roi and his murder of that monarch; and his courtship of Emer.

Cuimne, the hag who assisted Mongan in recovering his wife.

Culan, a smith who forged a sword, spear and shield for Conor. He may have been none other than Manannan. He is chiefly remembered for the fact that Cuchulain slew his dog.

Cumhal, the father of Finn and the husband of Murna. He was leader of the Fianna and was killed at the Battle of Knock. It has been suggested that the legend of Finn goes back to matriarchal times, as the Irish word *cumhal* signifies a 'bondmaid' or 'slave-girl'.

Cu Roi, a king of Munster who chose Cuchulain to be champion of Ireland. When his judgment was not accepted by Laoghaire and Conall Cearnach, he disguised himself as a giant and presented himself at Emhain Macha. He challenged each of the three to cut off his head and then to let him retaliate. Sure that no such retaliation would occur, the warriors agreed. However, when Laoghaire and Conall struck their blows the giant merely picked up his head. Neither would let him return the blow. When it came to Cuchulain's turn, he also failed to slay the giant but showed himself quite prepared to let himself be smitten, whereupon Cu Roi revealed his identity and confirmed Cuchulain as champion.

Later, raiding in Scotland, Cuchulain was aided by Cu Roi and they captured three cows, a cauldron and a lady named Blathnad. Cuchulain refused to share the booty, so Cu Roi seized the lot, buried Cuchulain up to his armpits and shaved off his hair. Cu Roi made Blathnad his wife, but she assisted Cuchulain to murder him.

Dabilla, the lapdog of Boann.

Da Derga's Hostel, a structure built on the River Dodder. It was beseiged by marauders when King Conaire was within. This monarch wrought great destruction on the attackers, but perished from thirst brought on by his endeavours in the course of fighting. Conall Cearnach was amongst his supporters but survived the fray.

Dagda, an important god of the pagan Irish who was later euhemerised into a leader of the Tuatha De Danaan. Dagda is, in fact, a title signifying 'good god'; his personal name was Eochaid U Oathair. He dressed after the fashion of a peasant and had a magic club, dragged on wheels. With one end of this weapon he could slay his enemies and with the other end he could heal those he had slain. A craftsman, when the Fomorians enslaved his people he built strongholds for them. A personage of great appetite, he was particularly fond of porridge.

Daire, a son of Finn, he was swallowed by a monster but cut his way out.

Daireann, a woman of the Sidhe (fairies), daughter of Bodb, who said she would marry Finn if the latter would have her as his only wife for a year and give her half his time thereafter. Finn refused, whereupon she gave him a cup of enchanted mead to drink which drove Finn insane, so that he railed at the Fianna, who deserted him, but Caoilte persuaded them to return and at nightfall the madness passed.

Dairine, daughter of Tuathal, king of Ireland, was the second wife of Eochu, king of Leinster.

Daithlenn, a hound of Mael Fhothartaig.

Daman, the father of Ferdia, he was one of the Firbolg.

Dana, the goddess from whom the Tuatha De Danaan took their name, sometimes confused with Anu.

Dathi, an early Irish king who reigned in the fifth century. According to tradition, he was the nephew of Niall of the Nine Hostages and the king of Connacht. On Niall's death he became king of Tara. He raided into Europe and came to a tower occupied by Formenius, king of Thrace. The Irishmen demolished the tower and, on a prayer by Formenius, a flash of lightning killed Dathi.

Dead Hand, the hand of a corpse, used by Irish witches.
With it they can still a well and skin a neighbour's milk
from its surface.

Dealgnaid, the wife of Partholon.

Deirdre, the daughter of Felimid, her story is reckoned one
of the three sorrowful tales of Ireland. It being
prophesied by Cathbad that she would grow to be
wondrously beautiful, Conor mac Nessa had her reared
apart from men, so that she would become his wife.
Levarcham the poetess was her guardian and, when
Deirdre was grown, she gave a prophetic description of
her future lover, whom Levarcham recognised as
Naoise, the son of Usnach. Deirdre went to Emhain
Macha and Naoise, seeing her, loved her. Fearful of
Conor, Naoise and his brothers fled with Deirdre,
travelling first about Ireland and then to Scotland, where
they took service with the king; but the king, apprised
by his steward of Deirdre's beauty, desired her so they
had to flee again. Conor lured them back to Ireland,
using Fergus mac Roi as his emissary. They stayed at
the lodging of the Red Branch and at first Conor left
them in peace, for Levarcham had told him untruly that

Deirdre, one of the best known figures in Irish mythology

Deirdre's beauty had faded; but through Arun the king discovered the deception and had the Red Branch attacked. The sons of Usnach were forced out by wizardry and slain by Maine, the king's underling, with one stroke of a sword given to Naoise by Manannan. At this Deirdre made great lamentation and then fled and stabbed herself, throwing the knife into the sea ere she died so that none should be blamed for her death.

Deluge, accounts of a great flood are found in the myths and legends of many countries. While J. G. Frazer thought the wide dispersal of such legends was due largely to Christian missionaries, other writers such as the French archaeologist, G. Roux, and the American Jesuit, J. L. Mackenzie, have suggested there may be an historical basis for the legends. The argument of L. Woolley, supported by R. Graves, that the Mesopotamian and Hebrew Deluge legends sprang from a local flood in the Tigris-Euphrates valley has no physical evidence to support it. The Irish have a legend of a great flood, but it is questionable whether or not this is of entirely Christian introduction. Certainly it has been influenced by the Old Testament narrative, but it has features of its own — the visit of Cesair to Ireland beforehand and the four survivors apart from Noah, notably Fintan, who turned himself into a salmon.

Derbrenn, Aengus's first love. She had six foster-children, turned into pigs by their mother. Maeve hunted them and slew them.

Der Greine, the daughter of Fiachna who married Laoghaire. Her name means 'tear of the sun'.

Dermot. 1. One of the Fianna, noted for his love spot. Grania, the betrothed of Finn, put a geas on him to elope with her and he complied. Finn pursued and eventually slew him.

2. A king of Tara, husband of Becfola. He once fought with Guaire and defeated him but them surrendered to him, for Guaire was a charitable person.

Dervorgill, the daughter of the king of Rathlin, she had been left for Fomorians in lieu of a tax payment. Cuchulain slew the Fomorians. Later, when he had returned to the mainland of Ireland, he shot down a bird with his sling. The bird turned into Dervorgill. Cuchulain sucked the stone out of her and gave her to one of his companions as a wife.

Diancecht, the god of healing, an important member of the Tuatha De Danaan. He killed his son, Miach, as a result of jealousy when Miach proved himself the better physician. He and his daughter Airmed guarded a spring of health, which restored dead or wounded members of the Tuatha De Danaan.

Digde, a name applied to the Cailleach Beara.

Dige, a name applied to the Cailleach Beara.

Dithorba, an opponent of Macha the Red, defeated by her.

Diuran, a poet and companion of Maeldun on his voyage.

Doilin, a hound of Mael Fhothartaig.

Donn. 1. The Brown Bull of Cuailgne so desired by Maeve. She and her husband Ailell were comparing their possessions, each contending his were more extensive than the other's. On discovering that Ailell had the bull Finnbheannach, of which she did not have the equal, Maeve desired Donn and over this the war between Connacht and Ulster was fought. When taken to Connacht by Maeve's forces, Donn fought with and slew Finnbheannach and then returned to his own country where he died. Donn and Finnbheannach were originally divine swineherds who had many incarnations as animals.

2. A son of Milesius and Seang.

3. The Irish god of the dead, perhaps identical with the Dagda, who resided at Teach Doinn, off the south-west coast. In modern folklore he is associated with shipwrecks, crops, cattle and sea-storms.

4. A foster-brother of Mael Fhothartaig. He slew Echaid and his wife and son in retaliation for Mael Fhothartaig's killing.

Dovinia, legendary ancestress of the Corcu Daibne of Kerry.

Druid, the word 'druid' — in modern Irish *draoi* — may originally have signified 'oak knower' or 'knower of a great deal'. They were the priesthood or at least part of the priesthood of the ancient Celts, being found in Britain and Gaul as well as Ireland and possibly also in Galatia. Julius Caesar's account of them is perhaps the best known one by a classical writer. Another well-known account by Posidonius may not be too historical. Whether the druids adhered to a single corpus of religious belief is doubtful, a certain diversity of doctrine seeming to be indicated by the study of Gaulish religion. Gaulish druidism may have been stamped out in A.D. 54, that of Britain perhaps later. In Ireland druidism persisted until the coming of Christianity. When Ireland had become a Christian society the niche formerly occupied by druids appears to have been filled by the *filid,* a word inadequately translated as 'poets'. Druids in Ireland may have formed an hereditary caste. Each king had a personal druid, but Keating tells us that when the kings were Christian a Christian chaplain replaced the druid.

According to one theory, druidism was a pre-Celtic British religion, taken over by the Celts and spread to the Continent. Druids were associated with the oak tree,

Quercus, and were said by Pliny to cut mistletoe, *Viscum album,* from it with a golden sickle on the sixth night of the moon. As gold is not sufficiently tough to accomplish this, it is possible that what was really employed was a sickle of gilded bronze. Druids were further associated with the oak because they ate acorns to make themselves ready to prophesy.

Druidess, druidesses are mentioned as existing in both Ireland and Gaul, but whether these were really female druids or merely women with some religious or magical function is uncertain.

Dubh, a wife of Enna, son of Nos. On discovering Enna had another wife, she, being a druidess, drowned her rival by magic but she was slain with a sling and fell into a pool. The pool was called Dubhlinn (Dubh-pool), modern Dublin, after her.

Dubh Lacha, the wife of Mongan and the daughter of Fiacha the Fair (also called Fiacha Lurgan) who is variously described as king of Dal Araide and king of Ulster.

Dubhlaing, the lover of Aoibhell. At the Battle of Clontarf she protected him with a covering of invisibility, but he cast it off. Aoibhell prophesied that he would die in the battle which he did.

Dubhthach, he assisted Fergus mac Roi in his attack on Conor after the slaying of the sons of Usnach.

Duineach, a name applied to the Cailleach Beara.

Dullahan, in Irish folklore a headless horseman who rides a headless horse. With his whip he will flick out the eyes of those who watch him. He carries his head with his cheese-coloured face beneath his arm. His horse has a detached head which precedes it. Dullahans can, in fact, put on and remove their heads. Sometimes they play ball, using their heads. They frequent churchyards. They have the endearing habit of throwing basins of blood in the faces of passers-by.

Dunlaing, a legendary king of Leinster who slew twelve ladies in Tara, which act was avenged by Cormac mac Art.

Durfulla, a daughter of the king of the merfolk who married one of the Cantillon family. When she died she was interred on an island which was the family's burial ground. This was then overrun by the sea. When a member of the family died, his body was left on the seashore and carried off by the merfolk until this was espied by a mortal, one Connor Crowe.

Eadon, the nurse of poets, one of the Tuatha De Danaan.

Echaid. 1. The foster-father of Lugh.

2. The King of Dunseverick. He gave his daughter in marriage to Ronan, king of Leinster, in the hope that

she would have an affair with Mael Fhothartaig. When the latter's death was caused by her, Donn slew Echaid, his wife and son.

Eel-Horse, a term applied to lake monsters.

Eibhir, a yellow-haired foreigner from a sunny country who married Ossian.

Eire, a goddess who requested the Tuatha De Danaan to give her name to Ireland, which they did.

Eirnin, the mother of Eire, Banba and Fodla, three goddesses who represented the country of Ireland.

A dullahan, a headless horseman who rides a headless horse

Eisirt, the poet of Iubdan, who laughed at that king's boast of the prowess of himself and his court, saying that the men of Ulster were giants compared with the little people. To prove his point, he went to the court of Fergus mac Leide and brought back Aedh, the dwarf, who seemed indeed a giant to the week folk. He then laid a geas upon Iubdan to go to Emhain Macha and be the first next morning to taste the porridge there. Eisirt was something of a prophet; he foretold that Iubdan would be held prisoner a year and a day by the Ulstermen, after which he would have to render up his dearest possession. He was also able, by some form of extra-sensory perception, to tell Fergus that he was having an affair with his steward's wife, just as Fergus's foster-son was having with his queen.

Eithne, the wife of King Ronan of Leinster and the mother of Mael Fhothartaig.

Emer, the wife of Cuchulain. Her father, Forgall, was opposed to the hero's marriage to her and managed to persuade him to undertake training with the woman warrior, Scathach. In his absence, Forgall tried to marry her off to a southern king, Lugaid mac Ros, but when the latter heard Cuchulain desired her, he grew fearful, so no marriage took place. On Cuchulain's return, he stormed Forgall's dun and carried her off.

Emhain Abhlach, an island paradise, perhaps Arran, off the coast of Scotland.

Emhain Macha, capital of Ulster at the time of Conor mac Nessa. It was supposed to have been called after twins born to Macha.

Enchanted Island, according to an eighteenth century work quoted by Wood-Martin, such an island was seen once a year floating off the coast of Antrim. It was believed that a sod of earth thrown on to it would make it stable.

Eochaid O Uathair, the name of the Dagda.

Eochu, a legendary king of Leinster who married Fithir, the daughter of Tuathal Techtmar. However, returning to his kingdom, his subjects assured him that Fithir's younger sister, Dairine, was a better proposition, so he took her as his second wife, whereupon Fithir died of shame and Dairine died of grief. Tuathal levied war on Leinster and Eochu was slain. His son Erc succeeded him but the Leinstermen had to pay a tribute.

Eoghan. 1. A king of Connacht, mortally wounded fighting the Ulstermen. He said he was to be buried on the Connacht border, facing Ulster, and that he would protect his kingdom, but the Ulstermen later dug him up and buried him face downward near Lough Gill.

2. Alternative name of Mug Nuadat.

3. An exile from Ireland who married Beara, the daughter of the king of Spain.

Eolas, one of Partholon's three druids.

Er, a son of Partholon.

Eri, a queen of the Tuatha De Danaan, said to have given her name to Ireland. She was the wife of Cethor.

Esa, the daughter of Etain and Eochaidh.

Etain, the wife of Midir. Another of Midir's wives, Fuamach, in jealousy turned her into a fly. She was swallowed by the wife of Etar and reappeared as a baby. When she grew up, she married the high king Eochaidh. Midir stole her away and they departed in the guise of swans. Eochaidh attacked Midir's hill of Bri Leith and recaptured her.

Etarlaim, a druid, the lover of Fuamach. The latter was one of the wives of Midir who, for her adultery, slew her.

Eterscelae, legendary king of Tara, husband of Mess Buachalla.

Ethlinn, the daughter of Balor and the mother, by Cian, of Lugh.

Fafne, the brother of Aige. After her death at the hands of Meilge's warriors, he satirised the king so that three blotches appeared on him. For this he was executed.

Fairy, the word usually employed to translate the Irish *Sidhe*. In Ireland fairies are either diminutive beings, such as the leprechaun, or beings of normal human stature. These latter are of both sexes. They go about in troops. They have the gift of healing, which they can pass on the humans. Sometimes a mortal may be sought by a fairy lover *(leannan sidhe)*. If he refuses her advances, he is her master; if he succumbs she dominates him. Fairies live in mounds.

Fairy Dog, such a creature, with a white ring around his neck, has been reported in the vicinity of Galway.

Fand, an Irish goddess, the wife of Manannan. She fought against him and three demons attacked her kingdom. Cuchulain defeated them and she became his mistress. Emer, discovering this, came to slay her husband, but Manannan took Fand back. Cuchulain was given a draught of forgetfulness to ease the pain of his loss.

Faolan, the son of a foreign woman who had come to Ireland to be Finn's lover. He became a member of the Fianna.

Faruach, a son of the king of Innia. He could magically make a ship by striking three blows with his axe on his sling.

Fathadh Canaan, one who obtained dominion over the entire world, taking hostages from the birds, the streams and the languages.

Fear Gorta, a spectre found in time of famine. It begs for alms and, if its entreaties prove successful, rewards the giver. Its name means 'man of hunger'.

Feda, the first of the followers of Partholon to die in Ireland.

Fedelm, a fairy, the lover of Cuchulain.

Fedelma, a prophetess who told Maeve her expedition against Ulster would be defeated.

Feenish, the mare of Captain Macnamara. Because he had rubbed her with a magic stone, she possessed human intelligence. She died when, after a strenuous day, her master made her swim the river at Cong. She was buried at Inis Feenish in Lough Corrib.

Fe Fiada, a somewhat mysterious object or power which rendered the Irish fairies invisible.

Feinius Farsaidh, a king of Scythia who established a school on the Plain of Shinar. He was father of Neanul, who succeeded him, and of Niul.

Feis, a feast held at Tara, perhaps originally to celebrate the marriage of the king to the earth goddess, as the word is the gerund of Old Irish *fo-aid,* 'to sleep with'.

Ferann, a son of Partholon.

Fercherdne, the poet of Cu Roi, who avenged him by killing his wife, Blathnad.

Ferchertne, a poet, companion of Labraid.

Ferdia, a friend of Cuchulain who fought on the Connacht side in the war over the Brown Bull. Maeve goaded him into fighting Cuchulain and, on the fourth day of their combat, Cuchulain slew him.

Fer Ferdiad, a druid of the Tuatha De Danaan, sent by Manannan to lure Tuage for him. Disguised as a woman, Fer Ferdiad lulled her to sleep and brought her to Inbhear Glas, where he left her to look for a boat. There she was drowned and the angry Manannan slew Fer Ferdiad.

Fergna, a son of Partholon.

Fergoman, a member of the Fianna.

Fergus. 1. Fergus the Black-toothed was a legendary high king of Ireland who came from Ulster and who was defeated by Cormac mac Art, who succeeded him.

2. The name of two brothers of Fergus the Black-toothed: Fergus the Long-haired and Fergus the Fiery.

3. A son of Nemed.

4. A poet, a member of the Fianna, called 'fairmouth'.

Fergus Mac Leide, an Irish king who encountered the Muirdris beneath Lough Rury. His face became twisted in fright, a state of affairs which was permanent. Such a blemish should have deprived him of his throne but his subjects, who revered him, hid all mirrors so that he would not discover what was the matter with him. A servant girl at length revealed the truth. Fergus returned to Lough Rury, slew the Muirdris and died. Fergus also featured in the story of Iubdan and Eisirt.

Fergus Mac Roi, a king of Ulster, who married Ness, mother of Conor. She tricked him into surrendering his kingdom to her son. When Maeve made war on Ulster, Fergus took the Connacht side.

Feron, an Irish legend, a survivor of the Deluge.

Fiachna, a fairy man, the son of Retach, his wife was abducted. He slew her abductor whose nephew, Goll, then took her and defeated Fiachna in seven battles when he tried to regain her. He eventually regained her with the aid of Laoghaire.

Fiachra, a son of Lir.

Fiacra, a son of Conor mac Nessa killed by Conall Cearnach.

Fianna, a band of legendary soldiers — their name means 'wild animals' — of whom Finn mac Cool was the most celebrated leader. They were finally routed at the Battle of Gabhra by the forces of a hostile high king.

Findabair, the daughter of Ailell and Maeve who was in love with Fraoch.

Finegas, a poet who watched for the Salmon of Knowledge, hoping to catch and eat it. Finn became his pupil and, when the poet caught the fish, he gave it to Finn to cook. Finn burnt his finger on it, sucked the burn and thereby gained some of the knowledge. Finegas, realising his alumnus was destined to eat the salmon, gave him the rest of it.

Fingal, a name used in Scotland for Finn, made well-known by Macpherson, although calling Finn Fingal was something which was certainly done as early as the fourteenth century. Fingal is actually a separate name, meaning 'fair foreigner', whereas Finn just means 'fair'. The name Fingal was borne by a king of Man and the Isle who reigned from 1070 to 1077, which shows that it was actually employed.

Fingel, the mother of Noidhiu. When he was born she wanted him slain, but he pronounced the nine judgements and thus preserved himself.

Finn. 1. One of the most celebrated Irish heroes was Finn mac Cool. He may originally have been an aspect of the god Lugh. He is likely at any rate to have once been regarded as a god, equating to the Welsh Gwyn ap Nudd and perhaps having a Continental equivalent also, whose name is commemorated in such cities as Vienna (Latin *Vindobona*).

The story of Finn as we have it, however, depicts a hero who is regarded as having flourished in the time of Cormac mac Art. His father, Cumhal, was leader of the Fianna. He was defeated by Clan Morna under Goll at the Battle of Knock, where he met his death. Finn's mother entrusted him to the care of two women, Bodhmall the druidess and Liath Luachra. When Finn grew up he recovered the Treasure Bag of the Fianna. He placed himself under the tutelage of Finegas on the banks of the Boyne. There he consumed a Salmon of Knowledge, gaining wisdom, more of which valuable commodity he obtained from Beag's well of the moon.

He came to the court of the high king and there slew a man of the Tuatha De Danaan, who was wont to lull the folk of Tara to sleep with sorcerous music and then set the place afire.

Finn became, with Goll's consent, head of the Fianna. His exploits involved hunting, fighting and sorcery. His hounds, Bran and Sceolan, were his own nephews, offspring of his bewitched sister. His son Ossian was the child of a woman transformed into a deer. He is a principal character in the tale of Dermot and Grania. The Battle of Ventry, fought against Daire Donn, high king of the World, was one of the great military events of his career.

Accounts of Finn's death are very vague. Perhaps in the original story, in which Finn was a god, nothing was known of his demise. One tale makes the sons of Uigreann his killers.

According to one tale, Finn still survives, sleeping in a cave. This is an Irish version of the widespread Sleepers legend, also told of such persons as King Arthur, Frederick Barbarossa and Owen Llawgoch. A Christian variant may exist in the legend of the Seven Sleepers of

Finn was drowned in the lough subsequently named after her

Ephesus. This legend perhaps dates back to prehistoric times, when a king was interred with his retainers.

Folklore sometimes made Finn a giant. He was credited with building the Giant's Causeway in County Antrim.

2. The sister of Fergoman. When the latter was dying, wounded by a son, she, standing on a lakeside, heard the echo of his cries. She swam towards it, but on reaching the far side, she heard his cries, now on the other side. Perplexed, she swam back and forth, always hearing the cries on the opposite side, until she drowned. The lake was called Lough Finne after her.

3. The name of a son of Ossian and Niamh.

4. This Finn, called Finn the White, the son of Brasil, was a member of the Fianna.

5. The name of three brothers of Maeve, sons of Eocaidh Feidleach, king of Tara.

Finnbheannach, a bull, born in the herds of Maeve, who, deeming it unfit that he should be ruled by a woman, transferred himself to the herds of Ailell. He was slain by Donn, the Brown Bull of Cuailgne. These bulls may originally have been divine figures, such as Deotaros, the Celtic divine bull recorded in Asia Minor.

Fintan, this personage was the husband of Cesair, whom he abandoned. He survived the Deluge by turning into a salmon and lived until a great age. Indeed, he was a witness in a lawsuit of the sixth century.

Fionnuala, a daughter of Lir.

Fios, one of Partholon's three druids.

Firbolg, a race of legendary inhabitants of Ireland who inhabited the country after the Nemedians but before the Tuatha De Danaan. They may represent the genuine pre-Gaelic population of the country.

Fithir, a daughter of Tuathal, king of Ireland, who married Erc, king of Leinster.

Flood, *see* Deluge.

Fochmart, one of Parthalon's three druids.

Fodla, an early Irish goddess, who met the invading Tuatha De Danaan and asked them that they give her name to Ireland, which they did.

Foltlor, a son of the king of Innia, who could follow any track on land or sea. He assisted the Fianna in the adventure of the Giolla Deacar.

Fomorians, a race of demons who had their headquarters on Tory Island. They fought with the Partholonians, Nemedians and Tuatha De Danaan, sometimes enslaving the country. Their leaders included Balor, Conaing, Morc and Cical. Some of them had only a single hand and foot. The meaning of their name is perhaps the prefix *fo-*, 'under', and a root word meaning something like 'demon'.

Forgall, the father of Emer, who opposed Cuchulain's union with her. He was killed when Cuchulain attacked his dun.

Formenius, the king of Thrace whose prayer caused Dathi to be struck by lightning. Formenius seems unknown outside Irish legend: perhaps his name is a version of Faramund, mentioned by the Frankish chronicler Fredegar.

Fors, in Irish legend, a survivor of the Deluge. He was the son of Electra, son of Seth. He died in Jerusalem in the year Christ was born.

Fraoch, a hero, son of Bebind and nephew of Boann. He loved Findabair, daughter of Ailell and Maeve, but he could not persuade her to elope with him, nor would he pay the bride price her parents demanded. While he was swimming, Ailell told him to bring him a rowan branch from the bank. He did so but, on being sent back for more, a monster attacked him. He fought the monster, aided by Findabair who jumped into the water with his sword. He killed the creature and, wounded, was taken off and tended by the fairies. Next day he returned and Findabair's parents gave their consent to the wedding.

Freagarthach, 'answerer', the sword of Manannan. Its every wound was mortal.

Fuamach, the first wife of Midir who was so anxious to destroy Etain.

Gae Bolga, the spear of Cuchulain.

Gael. 1. A son of Niul who dwelt in Egypt.

2. The son of Eatnor who, on Feinius Farsaidh's instructions, arranged and divided the Gaelic language. The actual derivation of the word 'Gael' (Old Irish *Goidel*) is probably from Brythonic.

Gamal, a door-keeper at Tara in the reign of Nuada.

Gan Ceann, a headless creature in folklore.

Ganconer, an amorous leprechaun-like being, idle by nature, who is to be found in lonely valleys and who makes love to milkmaids and shepherdesses.

Gathelus, alternative form of Gael.

Geas, a bond or taboo, which, when placed upon someone, forced that person to obey the instruction given him. The most famous geas (plural *geasa)* of Irish legend was perhaps the one Grania placed on Dermot to make him elope with her.

Gebann, a druid and the father of Cliona.

Gelban, a son of the king of Lochlann who, at Conor's behest, looked into the House of the Red Branch to see if Deirdre's beauty had really faded. Deirdre spotted him and Naoise knocked out one of his eyes with a fidchell piece, but he nonetheless reported to Conor that she was still beautiful.

Fraoch, the nephew of Boann, was aided by his beloved, Findabair, when a monster attacked him

Gerald, Earl of Desmond, an historical personage who died in 1583. According to legend, he was a sorcerer and the son of Aine. One of his early magical feats was to jump into a battle. His wife pleaded with him to demonstrate his powers and he changed, first into a vulture, then a hag, then a snake. Then, having turned back to his original form, he stretched nearly from one end to the other of the huge room where this demonstration was taking place. His wife screamed and the whole castle sank beneath Lough Gur and there the earl is said to lie enchanted, coming up once in seven years and riding a silver shod horse.

Germane, a companion of Maeldun on his voyage.

Giant, a human of very great size. Giants occur in Irish legend. One of the Irish words for a giant is *athach*, which also means 'a churl', so in Irish imagination a giant may be thought of as a great, loutish rustic. Finn came to be regarded as a giant in later legend. One theory about the widespread belief in giants in Europe is that they are a reminiscence of Neanderthal men who fought with Cro-Magnon adversaries. Another explanation may be in the finding of large bones of prehistoric animals and their being regarded as the remnant of gigantic humans. Sometimes races of small stature may have regarded taller folk as giants. A purely literary race of giants was that of Brobdingnag, created by the Irish writer, Jonathan Swift. Another Irish writer, C. S. Lewis, made use of giants in his Narnian stories, particularly *The Silver Chair* (1953).

Gille Greine, she was the daughter of a human father and a sunbeam. When told this, she jumped into Lough Greine (the lake of the sun), floated to Derry Graney (the oak-grove of the sun) and was buried in Tuam Graney.

Giolla Deacar, a giant who, claiming to be the world's worst servant, enlisted as a servant of Finn. He claimed Finn's protection for his horse, which proved to be of pugnacious temperament and attacked the Fianna's horses. Conan, seeing it about to attack his own animals, put a halter on it and tried to ride it, but was unable to make it go. His fellow Fenians suggested he wasn't heavy enough, so no fewer than fourteen more got on its back. The Giolla Deacar now left and the steed left with him. The riders were unable to get off and Liagan, running behind, caught its tail and was unable to let go. They all went into the sea which parted before them and closed behind them, so the Fianna were unable to follow them. Finn and his followers, aided by Faruach, who could make a ship magically, and Foltlor, a tracker, had to go in quest of them. Eventually they found them. It transpired that the Giolla Deacar was Abarta, one of the Tuatha De Danaan. Peace was made between the parties and the prisoners released, but Conan demanded, as satisfaction, that fifteen of Abarta's followers should ride the horse back to Ireland and that Abarta himself should follow, holding its tail. To this Abarta agreed.

Goatheads, a monstrous race of beings, perhaps a part of the Fomorian race.

Goban Saor, an euhemerised version of the god Goibniu, who survives in Irish folklore, where he is depicted as a wandering architect, the builder of round towers, cathedrals and churches.

Goibniu, an important god of the early Irish. In modern folklore he would appear to have survived as the character called 'the Goban Saor'.

Golamh, the original name of Milesius. It means 'soldier', just as Milesius's Irish name, *Mile,* means 'warrior', from the Latin *miles*.

Goll, an important member of the Fianna, involved with

those who defeated Finn's father, Cumhal. When Finn came to power, Goll accepted him as leader of the Fianna. He eventually slew Finn's son, Cairell, and, when Oscar tried to heal matters between Finn and him, he, mistaking Oscar's intentions, flung a spear at him. He was trapped by Finn's men and died after twelve days, apparently from lack of food.

Gorm Glas, the sword of Conor mac Nessa.

Gortighern, the language spoken by all mankind before the confusion of tongues at the Tower of Babel. It later became Hebrew.

Grania, the lover of Dermot

Grania, the lover of Dermot, who fled with him from Finn, to whom she had been affianced.

Grian, a fairy queen with a court at the top of Pallas Green

Hill, County Tipperary. Her name may mean the same as the Modern Irish *grian*, 'sun', perhaps indicating a solar divinity behind the legend.

Gruagach, an Irish word signifying 'ogre', 'giant' or 'wizard'; in Omeath it was used to mean a champion. It appears to be derived from *gruaig*, 'hair', and perhaps originally denoted a manlike, hairy monster, possibly of the same kind as the Anglo-Saxon woodwose, the Tibetian yeti, the North American sasquatch and oh-ma and those 'wild men' closely related by nature to the giants of which J. Grimm speaks.

Hag of Beare, see *Cailleach Beara.*

Hag of the Finger, a crone who had a gigantic son. She could be slain only with a silver arrow. Her killing was accomplished by Finn.

Hallowe'en, *see Samhain.*

Ham, the son of Noah. In Irish legend, he was the ancestor of the leprechauns, Fomorians and goatheads.

Head, as is attested by sculpture, the head seems to have had a pagan cultic significance amongst the Celts, both on the Continent and in Ireland.

Heber, a son of Milesius who, after the Milesian conquest of Ireland, obtained the two provinces of Munster and gave of his territory to his brother Amergin.

Heremon, a son of Milesius who, after the Gaelic conquest, was given Connacht and Leinster.

High King, before the Norman Conquest (1169), Ireland was divided into a number of kingdoms, with a paramount high king *(ard-righ)*. The high kingship only effectively existed from about the time of Malachy I, but later legend and pseudo-history were to claim it had existed right back into prehistoric times. In fact, the corpus of early Irish law — termed the Brehon Laws — makes no proper allowance for the position of a high king at all; but the possibility that there existed some form of sacral kingship of the island at Tara in pagan times has been suggested.

Hill of the Wave, the hill to which Fintan fled, when, after the death of Bith and Ladra, he was the only man left in Ireland and the women of the others were coming to join him. According to another source, Banba survived the Flood on top of this hill.

Horse, this animal is believed to be frequently annoyed by fairies.

Horse-Eel, a term applied to lake monsters.

Horseshoe, the shoes of horses and donkeys are deemed lucky if found and nailed to a doorpost. In the case of the donkey this was perhaps because of its presence at the Nativity. The original belief may have been that the horseshoe, made of iron, warded off otherworld beings.

Hungry Grass, this grows where a victim of the Great Famine died. If you cross it by night you will be seized by a hunger which will kill you unless you appease it immediately.

Hy-Brasil, a legendary Atlantic island supposed to lie to the west of Ireland and to become visible every seven years. O'Flaherty writes of a contemporary named O'Ley who claimed to have been kidnapped and taken to the island. The name of this island in due course began to appear on maps, the first such, placing it in the latitude of the south of Ireland, being that of the Genoese cartographer, A. Dalorto, which appeared in 1325. It has been suggested that Hy-Brasil is a sunken land of which the Aran Islands are a remnant.

Iarbanel, a son of Nemed who was also a prophet.

Ibath, the son of Beothach and ancestor of the Tuatha De Danaan, he went to Boeotia from Ireland after the defeat of the Nemedians by the Fomorians. Another tradition states he went to Northern Europe.

Ibcan, a grandson of Nemed.

Ilbrec, a son of Manannan.

Imbolg, the pagan Irish spring festival, which occurred on 1 February. In Christian times it came to be celebrated as Saint Brigid's Day.

Immortality, no account of pagan Irish belief in immortality has been preserved, but a classical writer states that the Celts held a firm belief in life after death. The Rees brothers contend the stories of Irish voyages may originally have been a set of instructions relating to life after death.

Incubus, or demon lover was a feature of mediaeval legend. The incubus was said to be male — one such was Merlin's father — and the succubus or succuba female. We find the notion of a phantasmal lover in Ireland occurring in the story of Fingel. The succubus is paralleled by the notion of the fairy lover.

Indech, a Fomorian killed at the Second Battle of Moytura.

Invisibility, according to Irish folk belief, could be achieved by cutting a dead raven's heart three times, placing a bean in each rent, burying the heart and, when the beans sprouted, putting one in one's mouth and reciting a verse. Then, as long as the bean was in one's mouth, one remained invisible. The beans had to be black and the knife used to cut open the heart had to have a black handle.

Iollan, a son of Fergus mac Roi who defended the sons of Usnach when they were attacked by the Ulstermen. He had knocked down Fiacra and was on top of him with only the Ochain between them when Conall Cearnach, in response to the shield's bellowings, came and stabbed him. Iollan, before dying, told Conall of Conor's treachery towards the sons of Usnach, whereupon Conall slew Fiacra. Iollan and Fiacra had been born on the same day.

Ir, a leader of the Milesians, killed by a magic storm conjured up by the Tuatha De Danaan to oppose the Milesian landing in Ireland. He was a son of Milesius.

Irish Crocodile, a creature which, according to O'Flaherty, was to be found in Lough Mask.

Iubdan, a king of the little people, who, because of a geas laid on him by Eisirt, had to go to the court of Fergus mac Leide and be the first to sample the porridge there next morning. Accompanied by his consort, Bebo, he attempted to do this and, as a result, fell into the porridge pot and so was made prisoner by the Ulstermen. His people tried to obtain his release, first by offering a ransom of corn, then, on this being refused, by making the calves take all the milk from the cows, by defiling the rivers and wells, by burning the mills and kilns and by cutting the ears off the corn. At length they threatened to shave the Ulstermen and women in their sleep, whereupon Fergus told them he would kill Iubdan if this design were carried out. Iubdan then sent his subjects home. He remained prisoner a year and a day and then had to surrender his most precious possession — a pair of shoes — to Fergus. When Fergus put his toes into these, they grew to a size to fit his feet. Like Eisirt, Iubdan was able to prophesy.

Iuchar, a son of Tuireann.

Iucharba, a son of Tuireann.

Iunsa, the father of Eibhir, the wife of Ossian.

Jack, an hypocoristic form of the name John. It is commonly found as the name of the protagonist of English folk-tales and has been recorded as such in Irish folklore.

Jackdaw, a well-known bird, *Corvus monedula*. According to Kerry tradition, those of Kilgarvan could once talk. To escape the unwelcome attention of the crows they asked if they could move into the towns. At first, due to the opposition of the chief druid, the king said, 'No', but later, when a jackdaw found his missing ring and thereby saved Munster from a Fomorian attack, he relented. It is possible to teach a jackdaw to talk and this may have given rise to the story.

Jasconius, the name of the whale on whose back Saint Brendan and his followers landed, thinking he was an island. The name is derived from the Irish word *iasc*, 'fish'.

John the Baptist, a New Testament personage. According

to an hagiological legend recorded by Lady Wilde, his head became hard until it became the stone at Saint John's Well, County Cork.

King of the Cats, a garrulous feline, said to live in a cave near Clonmacnoise. If a person were to cut off a piece of his ear, it was said he would speak.

King of the Great Plain, an invader of Ireland, killed by Conn Cribher.

King of the Plain of Wonder, a monarch who gave Dermot his cup to heal the daughter of the King-Under-Wave.

Knock, the scene of the battle where Cumhal was killed by Clan Morna.

Labraid Loingseach, a legendary prehistoric king of Ireland. He was originally called Maen because he was dumb, due to eating a mouse. However, he was struck in a hurling match and emitted a cry, whereupon it was said that he was talking *(labraid)*. He was the son of Ailell, the king of Munster murdered by Cobthach. With the harper Craiftine and the poet Ferchertne he went to

According to Kerry tradition, the jackdaws of Kilgardan used to be able to talk

Scoriath, king of Fir Morca, of whose daughter he became enamoured. Scoriath and his wife were lulled to sleep by Craiftine's music so Labraid was able to meet the girl, whose name was Moriath. Moriath's mother, however, guessed what had happened. On Labraid's admitting his deed, he was allowed to wed Moriath. With the aid of Scoriath he took the Leinster stronghold of Dinn Rig, aided by Craiftine's sleep-music. When he was king of Leinster, he invited Cobthach to visit him and enter a house which he had built. Cobthach consented to this, provided Labraid's mother and fool should precede him. They did so and Cobthach followed them. Then Labraid had the house chained closed and cooked Cobthach in the house.

Labraid had, according to one account, become an exile in Britain and Armenia. This earned him the name 'Loingseach', the exile. He had everyone who cut his hair slain, for he had horse's ears and wanted to keep them secret. Yielding to the pleas of one barber's mother, he said he would spare her son provided he would hold his tongue. However, weighed down by the burden of his secret, the youth imparted it to a tree. The tree was later made into a harp for Craiftine and, on being played, it revealed the truth.

Ladra, an early settler in Ireland at the time of the daughters of Cain. According to another legend, Ladra accompanied Cesair in her ship to Ireland and was the first man to die there.

Laeg, the charioteer of Cuchulain.

Laiglinni, a son of Partholon.

Laoghaire. 1. A son of King Crevan of Connacht. He assisted Fiachna, a fairy man, to regain his wife from his nephew and went to live among the fairies, marrying Fiachna's daughter, Der Greine.

2. Legendary king of Ireland, brother of Cobthach, who murdered him.

3. An Ulster champion, companion to Cuchulain.

Leprechaun, a solitary fairy, a shoemaker or tailor, resembling a small man, of irascible temperament. The leprechaun is said to have a crock of gold, which he must surrender to whomsoever catches him. The etymology of the word is usually given as a compilation of *lugh*, 'small', and *corpan,* a diminutive of *corp,* 'body'.

Levarcham, the poetess and guardian of Deirdre who taught her all her skill.

Lia Fail, the stone of destiny, used as a coronation stone at Tara by the kings there. It was a phallic symbol and was called 'the stone penis'. It cried out when it touched the king-to-be. Fergus mac Erca was said to have brought it to Scotland, where it became the Stone of Scone, the coronation stone of the Scottish kings. However, there is a stone at Tara today which is known as the Lia Fail and this would seem to clash with this account. The first definite mention of the Scottish Stone of Scone is in 1249.

Liagan, a member of the Fianna and a great runner.

Liban, a mermaid associated with Lough Neagh. This lake was formed when, due to neglect of a holy well, the water escaped. Liban was preserved beneath the waves. However, she was captured, according to the *Annals of the Four Masters,* in 558.

Lir married Aoife, who turned his children from his previous marriage to Aobh into swans

Lir, one of the Tuatha De Danaan who had, by his wife Aobh, three sons, Aedh, Fiachra and Conn, and a daughter, Fionnuala. When Aobh died, he married Aoife, who turned her stepchildren into swans, in which shape they remained until the time of Saint Mochaomhog. By him, they were kept until King Lairgen of Connacht tried to seize them, whereupon they changed into humans, now aged after the passage of so many years. The saint baptised them before they died.

Lobais, the druid of the Fomorians.

Lochlann, in mediaeval Ireland, signified 'the country of the Norseman', but before the Viking incursions it may have been a legendary, superhuman country. The Welsh Llychlyn may have been its equivalent.

Loch Ness Monster, of which Saint Adamnan, a mediaeval Irish writer, in his *Life of Saint Columba,* reports an encounter of the saint with a monster in Loch Ness in Scotland. The monster was pursuing a swimmer, but, on being addressed by the saint, withdrew. This is the first recorded alleged sighting of a monster in Loch Ness. In modern times, since the construction of a new road by the loch, a considerable number of people have reported seeing a monster therein.

Lomna, the fool of the Fianna who betrayed an adulterous affair of one of Finn's wives to Finn and was murdered for his pains by her partner. He was avenged by Finn.

Lot, the mother of Cical. Her lips were in her breast, she had four eyes in her back and she was equal to her troop of followers in strength.

Lough Derg, no salmon are found in this lake in County Donegal. According to legend, this was because of a curse put on it by Saint Patrick.

Lough Derg Monster, a large monster which Saint Patrick compelled to go to the bottom of this County Donegal lake. It had formerly been on the shore, where it had been wounded by Finn, who had struck it in its vulnerable spot — a mole on its left side — with a spear, so that its blood had given a red tinge to the water of the lake. The monster had originated as a hairy worm in the thigh-bone of the dead Hag of the Finger. When it emerged, Conan threw it into the lake, whereupon it came out as a monster. According to another tradition, Conan himself killed it.

Lough Graney Monster, there was supposed to be a monster in the lough which appeared but once every seven years.

Lough Gur, a lake in County Limerick. According to legend it was once dry land. There was a well in it. This was neglected and overflowed, forming the lake. Every seven years it appears dry. Then a tree, covered with green cloth, can be discerned in it. The guardian of the well was the Toice Bhrean.

Lough Ree, there was said to be an underwater city in this lake. A bishop, hearing it contained a cathedral, went to visit it but never returned.

Lough Ree Monster, according to the *Life of Saint Mochuda,* this creature devoured a man. A sighting of a monster in this lake was reported in 1960.

Love Spot, no heart was impervious of this, called in Irish *ball seirce,* which belonged to Dermot. It was because of his love spot that Grania fell for him.

Luchtar, the carpenter of the Tuatha De Danaan.

Lugh, an important Irish god, equating to the British Lleu and the Continental Lugos. He arrived in Ireland when the Tuatha De Danaan were subjected to the Fomorians. These he helped defeat and, with his sling, he slew Balor, his own grandfather, who was one of their leaders. He later became the father of Cuchulain.

Lughnasadh, a festival which obviously takes its name from the god Lugh. It was supposedly introduced by him to commemorate his foster-mother Tailtiu but may, in fact, have been to mark the ritual wedding of the king to Eire, the eponymous goddess of Ireland. General wedding arrangements by parents for their children may have been a feature of the festival.

Lycanthropy, in psychology, is a condition wherein a man imagines himself to be an animal. In mythology, it is the actual turning of a man into an animal. Tales of lycanthropy occur in Irish legend, notably in the case of witch-hares. Giraldus Cambrensis mentions werewolves in Ossory. Tuirean was a were-bitch.

Mac An Daimh, the companion of Mongan, in his efforts to regain Dubh Lacha.

Mac Cuill, the slayer of Lugh.

Mac Datho, a king of Leinster, owner of a hound coveted by King Conor of Ulster and Ailell and Maeve, the king and queen of Connacht. He promised it to each and invited both parties to collect it on the same day. A pig was the principal dish of the feast. Bricriu suggested it should be divided according to martial accomplishments and Cet challenged anyone to contend with him for it or else he would divide it. Then Conall Cearnach arrived and said he was the greater warrior, which Cet admitted, but he assured Conall that his brother Anluan was a better warrior than either, whereupon Conall produced Anluan's head and flung it at Cet, so that the latter had to retire.

Mac Glas, the fool of Mael Fhothartaig, who was killed with his master.

Macha, the name of three women in Irish legend, these may originally have been the same personage, one of the major goddesses of Irish mythology. The first was the wife of Nemed, the first of his people to die in Ireland, and her name was given to Armagh, *Ard Macha,* or Macha's Height. Macha, the wife of Crunnchu the peasant, appeared mysteriously and brought him prosperity, but, because of a foolish wager on his part, she had to enter a foot race when pregnant. She gave birth, as a result, to twins, after which *Emhain Macha,* Macha's Twins was called and, dying, cursed the Ulstermen, so they suffered the sickness of childbirth when Ulster was in danger. The other Macha was a queen. Three men — Dithorba, Aedh and Cimbaeth — had been sharing the kingship, reigning alternately. On Aedh's death, the accession of his daughter, Macha the Red, was opposed by Dithorba and Cimbaeth, but she defeated them, married Cimbaeth and enslaved Dithorba's son and made them build the rampart of Emhain Macha.

Mac Ind Og, alternative name for Aengus, the love-god.

Macnamara, a villain who obtained supernatural powers in the following manner. He stole eggs from a raven's nest and boiled them. The raven brought a magic stone to its nest and revived its dead offspring. Macnamara stole the stone and rubbed himself with it. From this he acquired a number of extrasensory powers which stood him in good stead — those of foretelling the future, forcing others to do his will, etc. He also rubbed Feenish, his mare, with the stone and she acquired human intelligence. However, when she died Macnamara lost his powers.

Mael, a druid of Conn of the Hundred Battles.

Maeldun, according to a mediaeval Irish romance, he was the son of a chief slain by raiders. He determined to avenge his father's death and put to sea to do so. He was told to bring exactly sixty men with him, but his three foster-brothers managed to accompany him too. The following are the features of his voyage: (i) he came to an island where he overheard his father's assassin boasting of the deed, but, before he could effect a landing, his craft was swept away by a storm; (ii) the island of giant ants; (iii) a terraced island with coloured birds; (iv) an island containing an equine monster with dog's legs and blue claws; (v) the island of the demon horse race; (vi) an island of fighting equine animals; (vii) a walled island with a monster which could turn itself around inside its skin; (viii) an island of fiery animals; (ix) an island with a palace and a small cat; (x) an island divided by a brass wall with white sheep on one side and black sheep on the other; (xi) an island with a giant and a hot river; (xii) the island of the Miller of Hell; (xiii) an island of weeping black folk; (xiv) an island of walls of gold, silver, copper and crystal; (xv) an island with a crystal bridge over a fountain; (xvi) an island of speaking birds; (xvii) the island of a hermit with birds which were the souls of his descendants; (xviii) the island of giant smiths; (xix) a transparent sea; (xx) a country beneath waves; (xxi) an island with a watery wall; (xxii) an island with a stream which arched into the air; (xxiii) a silver pillar in the sea; (xxiv) a pillar supporting an island called Aoncos; (xxv) an island where the queen bade them remain and tried to make them stay; (xxvi) an island of intoxicating fruit; (xxvii) an island where a huge bird renewed his youth by bathing in a magic lake; (xxviii) an island of laughing people; (xxix) an island protected by a fiery wall; (xxx) a hermit emanating from Tory Island sitting on a rock; and (xxxi) a green island. Maeldun then came to the place where his enemy was, but that wight wished to make peace between them, to which course Maeldun was agreeable.

Mael Fhothartaig, the marvellous son of Ronan, king of Leinster. His stepmother made advances to him and, when he spurned them, falsely accused him to his father, who had him assassinated by Aedan. His sons avenged him by killing his slayer.

Maeltine, one of the Tuatha De Danaan, renowned for judgments.

Maen, the name, meaning 'dumb', once held by Labraid Loingseach.

Maer, a married lady who fell in love with Finn and sent him nine charm nuts to make him reciprocate her sentiments. Guessing their purpose, he refused to eat them.

Maeve. 1. The queen of Connacht, the wife of Ailell, when she found her possessions were not as extensive as her husband's she tried to procure the Brown Bull of Cuailgne from Ulster. When her efforts failed, she tried to take the bull by force. Her attack on Ulster led to the death of Cuchulain. Maeve may originally have been a goddess to whom it was necessary for the king to be ritually married. She therefore would appear to have been an early goddess, standing for the kingdom. She was said to have been the wife of nine kings and no one not married to her could reign. She had seven sons. Attempts to identify her with the English fairy queen Mab have not proven successful.

2. Maeve of the Red Side was a vague personage whom a king of Tara had to marry in order to reign.

Magh Mell, the pleasant plain, an Irish otherworld.

Magog, a Biblical personage. Irish tradition gave him three sons, Baabh, Iobath and Fathnachta. The latter was the ancestor of Partholon and Nemed and also of Attila the Hun.

Magpie, Lady Wilde avers there is no Irish name for this bird, a fact belied by Irish dictionaries. With regard to folk beliefs concerning it, she quotes the rhyme: 'One for sorrow/Two for mirth/Three for marriage/Four for a birth.' A variant of this is: 'One for sorrow/Two for joy/Three for a girl/Four for a boy.'

Maine. 1. A Norse prince who, at Conor's behest, killed the sons of Usnach. Naoise had killed his father and brothers.

2. The name borne by each of the seven sons of Ailell and Maeve.

Man, an island in the Irish Sea, taking its name from the sea-god Manannan and called in Irish *Inis Manannan,* 'the Isle of Manannan,' and in Latin *Monavia* or *Mona,* although the latter name was also applied to Anglesea. Manannan was supposed to come from Man and the island, whose inhabitants are Gaelic and akin to the Irish, was believed to be something of a paradise.

Manannan, the major sea god of the pagan Irish, equivalent of the Welsh Manawyddan. He would drive over the ocean and the waves would be as a plain to him. Later legend euhemerised him into a navigator from the Isle of Man. He ruled Tir Tairngiri. He was the father of Mongan whom he engendered by approaching the queen of Dal nAraidi when her husband was away at war and saying that, unless she bore him a son, the king would die. There is some similarity between this tale and that of the conception of Arthur. Manannan was a shape changer. His wife was Fand.

Marcan, the husband of Cred, perhaps the original of King Mark of Cornwall in Arthurian romance. Both their names may be connected with Celtic words for a horse.

Master-Otter, a large and legendary breed of otter. According to the legend, a house containing part of his skin cannot be burned. A man who has even an inch of it is impervious to wounds from bullet or steel.

Mathgen, the wizard of the Tuatha De Danaan.

May-Bush, on May Day such a bush was decorated with lighted candles, a survival, one assumes, of the May Day celebrations held at Beltane. A noted May-bush was at Swords, County Dublin.

Meabal, alternative name of Breg.

Mechi, the son of the Morrigan. He had three hearts with the shapes of three serpents through them. Had these grown they would have caused disaster in Ireland but Mechi was slain by Mac Cecht, an early ruler.

Meilge, the high king of Ireland who was satirised by Fafne.

Meng, alternative name of Breg.

Meran, a champion of Partholon.

Mermaid, a legendary sea-dwelling female, found in the folklore of many countries, including Ireland. Seals, manatees, dugongs and frustrated sailors' riotous imaginations may have all contributed to the growth of the legend. In Irish lore mermaids were found not only in the sea, but also in Lough Neagh. Saint Patrick was supposed to have turned old heathen women into mermaids. The *Annals of Ulster* and the *Annals of the Four Masters* both record a huge mermaid, the former stating that the year of her appearance was 890, the latter claiming it was 887. The Annals of Ulster record two more in 1118. Maurice Connor, the king of the

In Irish folklore mermaids were found not only in the sea, but also in Lough Neagh

pipers of Munster, was said to have gone beneath the
sea to live with a green-haired mermaid.

Merman, according to Irish lore, are creatures with green
teeth and hair. They have pigs' eyes and red noses.

Metempsychosis, the belief that after death the soul, having
left the body, enters another. The Celts seem to have
believed that after death the soul occupied another body
but in another world. It is, however, popularly thought
that they believed in reincarnation. There is no real
evidence of this, although some might hold that the story
of Tuan indicates that such a concept was not wholly
absent from the beliefs of the pagan Irish.

Miach, the son of Diancecht, the healer of the Tuatha De
Danaan. He was a better physician than his father. One
of his feats was to give a human an eye transplant from
a cat. His father had given Nuada a silver hand, but
Miach outdid him, restoring Nuada's fleshy hand. Seeing
his son to be the more proficient leech, Diancecht slew
him and herbs grew over his grave. His name may be
derived from the Latin word *medicus,* 'physician'.

Midir, one of the Tuatha De Danaan, husband of Etain and
Fuamach.

Milesians, the term applied to the Gaelic inhabitants of
Ireland, the last invaders of the country before the
historical period. The Irish Gaels belong to the Goidelic
branch of the Celtic race, linguistically distinguished
from the Britons or Brythonic branch known as p-Celts.
Mediaeval mythographers sought to make Milesians
ancestors of the non-Gaelic Erainn, perhaps in face
identical with the Firbolg, who were all too cognisant of
their non-Gaelic origins. By giving them a false pedigree,
the mythographers were able to fuse them with the
Gaels.

Milesius, a legendary Irish warrior whose Irish name, *Mile
Easpain,* represents a translation of the Latin *Miles
Hispaniae,* 'soldier of Spain'. Milesius was his later
name; his original name was Golamh, also supposed to
signify 'soldier'. The traditions concerning him are
largely, if not entirely, mediaeval fabrications. He was
one of the Scythians of Spain who returned to Scythia
and took service with the regnant king, Reafloir,
marrying his daughter Seang. Having grown fearful of
Milesius's might, Reafloir determined to kill him, but
Milesius killed his plotting father-in-law and left for
Egypt. Seang was dead but his sons, Donn and Airioch
Feabhruadh, accompanied him. He took service with
Pharaoh Nectanebus and was successful in war against
the Ethiopians. He married Scota, the daughter of
Nectanebus. They had two sons named Heber and
Amergin who were born in Egypt. They left Egypt and

another son, Ir, was born to them on the island of Irena, near Thrace. Colpa was born to them on the island of Gotia. Milesius returned to Spain where he defeated the Goths.

Mill, the first one in Ireland was erected in the reign of Cormac mac Art, who brought a millwright over from Scotland to perform the task.

Moling, a foster-brother of Finn, called 'the Swift'.

Mongan, an historical personage of the seventh century, said to have been the son of Manannan. According to one tradition he was a reincarnation of Finn mac Cool. He was reared by Manannan. He married Dubh Lacha, who had been born on the same night as he. He became a friend of Branduff, king of Leinster, and on one occasion promised Branduff anything he desired which it was within his power to give. Branduff demanded Dubh Lacha. Mongan was somewhat doubtful about this, but Dubh Lacha said it would be dishonourable to refuse. He did see her once again, however, changing his shape to that of a monk called Tibraide. Later on he tricked Branduff by turning up in the shape of the king's son of Connacht, accompanied by a hag named Cuimne, whom he made appear like the daughter of the king of Munster and to whom he gave a love charm. Branduff became enamoured of her and swapped Dubh Lacha for her. It was not until after Mongan's departure that the hag returned to her normal shape.

Mongfhinn, a sorceress, originally a goddess, who, having taken poison, died on Samhain Eve, on which date she was the recipient of prayers.

Moon Worship, it has been suggested that there is an element of moon worship (selenolatry) in Irish paganism because of the Irish custom of borrowing a piece of silver on the first night of a new moon. This was an omen of plenty for the forthcoming month. At the same time the borrower uttered a formula in Irish, 'As you found us in peace and prosperity, so leave us in grace and mercy'.

Morann, when Conor mac Nessa was undecided as to who would rear his nephew, Cuchulain, and when his underlings were disputing about this the matter was referred for judgment to Morann, who decreed that Sencha would teach him to speak, Fergus would dandle him and Amergin the warrior, would be his preceptor.

Morc, a Fomorian chief who came to Ireland from Africa after the death of Conaing and engaged the Nemedians in battle.

Moriath, the daughter of Scoriath, king of Fir Morca, who became the lover and later the wife of Labraid. Her mother's two eyes did not sleep at once; one of them was always keeping her under surveillance.

Mor Muman, in mediaeval legend, was a daughter of Aedh Bennan, an historical king of part of Munster. She was in reality a manifestation of the sun goddess.

Morrigan, an important goddess of the ancient Irish, a war and slaughter divinity, who helped the Tuatha De Danaan at Moytura and who fought with Cuchulain, having first tried unsuccessfully to tempt him to be her lover by turning into an eel, then into a wolf and then into a hornless red heifer. She may, in fact, have been a triune goddess, whose aspects were Morrigan, Badb and Macha (or Nemain). C. Kerenyi tells us the reason for such triune goddesses amongst the Greeks was that they represented the waxing, full and waning phases of the moon. This may have been true also of Ireland.

Mugain, the name of a number of persons in mediaeval Irish legend. They perhaps are euhemerised forms of a goddess of this name.

Mug Eime, the first lapdog ever to be introduced to Ireland was so called. It was obtained by a stratagem from Britain, despite a British law forbidding the export of lapdogs to Ireland.

Mug Nuadat, a legendary prehistoric king, the husband of a daughter of the king of Castile, who obtained the sovereignty of the southern half of Ireland by fighting against Conn of the Hundred Battles. A further war ensued over Mug Nuadat's wanting to share in the shipping customs of Dublin. He was killed fighting against Conn's forces at Moylena.

Muirdris, a name given to the lacustrine monster killed by Fergus mac Leide. It was also called 'the Sineach'.

Muirenn, the nurse of Cael, who provided him with a poem in praise of Credhe's possessions.

Muncnican, a champion of Partholon.

Murna, the mother of Finn mac Cool.

Nass, the wife of Lugh after whom Naas in County Kildare is named.

Nair, either a female spirit who consorted with Crevan or else his wife.

Naoise, the son of Usnach with whom Deirdre eloped.

Nar, the swineherd of Bodb Dearg.

Nath I, alternative form of Dathi.

Nechtan, was the husband of Boann and possibly an early water god.

Nemain, a war goddess of the pagan Irish whose name signified 'panic'. She was perhaps identical with Badb.

Nemanach, a son of Aengus the love-god.

Nemed, a descendant of Magog, son of Japhet, he sailed to Ireland from Scythia. He deforested a dozen plains in Ireland and defeated the Fomorians in three battles. He died of the plague on Great Island in Cork Harbour.

Nemedians, a race who came to Ireland with Nemed. They fought the Fomorians, at first successfully but were later defeated, some remaining in Ireland as a conquered people and the rest fleeing.

Nemedius, alternative form of Nemed.

Nera, a member of the household of Ailell, king of Connacht, who dwelt at Cruachan. On Samhain Eve, Ailell offered a price to whomsoever would encircle the foot of a recently hanged man with a withe. Nera did so and the corpse on the gallows asked him to take him down and give him a drink of water. Nera complied but, on returning, he saw Cruachan destroyed and the heads of the men of Cruachan held by the local fairy king, who pressed Nera into service. Nera married a woman of the fairies and she told him the destruction of Cruachan he had seen was an illusion but, unless the men of Connacht were warned, it would come true. Nera returned to Cruachan, warned Ailell, took his wife and child out of the fairy mound and Ailell attacked and destroyed it.

Nerbha, a daughter-in-law of Partholon.

Ness, the mother of King Conor of Ulster, she, by a subterfuge, obtained that kingdom from his predecessor, Fergus mac Roi. She agreed to marry Fergus only if he allowed her son Conor to reign in his stead for a year. He complied, but, when the year was over, she, supported by nobles she had won over, insisted that Conor retain the throne.

Net, an early Irish war god of whom little is known. He was the husband of Badb.

Nia, was made king of Connacht by Cormac mac Art, who was said to have been his half-brother.

Niall of the Nine Hostages, an historical king of Tara whose exact dates are uncertain but who flourished in the fifth century. According to legend, his mother was a Saxon princess. He was an ancestor of the Ui Neill dynasty.

Niamh, a princess of Tir na nOg who went to Ireland and persuaded Ossian to return with her to her country.

Niul, the son of Feinius Farsaidh and a renowned schoolmaster, who was invited by Cincris, Pharaoh of Egypt, to settle in his land. On friendly terms with the Israelites, this might well have caused friction between him and Cincris had not the latter perished when pursuing Moses across the Red Sea. He married Pharaoh Cincris's daughter, Scota, and their son was Gael.

Noidhiu, was a prodigious child. His mother, Fingel, was kept guarded lest she become pregnant, but a phantom impregnated her and, after nine months and nine years, she gave birth to Noidhiu, who at once uttered nine judgments, thus obtaining the name Noidhiu Naoi-mBreathach.

Noinden, a curse put upon Ulstermen by Macha

Noinden, a curse put on the Ulstermen by Macha. For nine times nine generations they would suffer the sickness of childbirth in time of crisis for Ulster. The curse was also attributed to Fedelm.

Nuada, an important god of the pagan Irish, euhemerised into a king of the Tuatha De Danaan. He suffered the loss of his hand and had, in consequence, to give up the kingship: he was replaced by Bres. Diancecht made him a silver hand, hence his being called *Argetlamh*. Miach made him one of flesh and blood and he was therefore able to resume the kingship.

O'Brazil, alternative name of Hy-Brasil.

Ochain, the magic shield of Conor mac Nessa. Whenever its bearer was in danger it roared, to be answered by Ireland's chief three waves — the Wave of Tuagh, the Wave of Cliona and the Wave of Rudraige.

Ogam, Ogham, the script of pre-Christian Ireland, its invention was ascribed to Ogma. It was at first used for inscriptions on vertical stones; later, in manuscripts, it was written horizontally. The alphabet was used often for ceremonial purposes and seems to have been particularly popular amongst the pre-Gaelic Erainn of West Munster. It contained letters such as q and z which do not occur in Modern Irish.

Ogma, a pagan Irish god, inventor of the Ogham alphabet and perhaps identical with the Gaulish god Ogmios, who was concerned with eloquence and was possibly also a psychopompos or conductor of souls.

Oillpheist, an Irish word meaning 'dragon' or 'great worm'. A creature of this sort, hearing that Saint Patrick was coming to drive out its kind, cut its way through the land, thus forming the River Shannon. On the way, it swallowed an inebriated piper named O'Rourke. Unabashed, O'Rourke continued to play his pipes to the monster's discomfort, so the creature expelled him.

Oirbsen, an alternative name for Manannan. Lough Corrib in County Galway used to be called Lough Oirbsen because Manannan was drowned there.

Oisin, *see* Ossian.

Omens, that belief in omens existed amongst the early Irish is attested by a story told by Giraldus Cambrensis — not an authority on whom one should rely. The frog *(Rana rana)* is not native to Ireland and, despite the large number of Irish names for it, such as *loscan, lispin, cronan dige,* was only introduced to the country in modern times. However, by some accident, Giraldus tells us, such an animal turned up in Ireland in the Middle Ages and the king of Ossory took it as an evil omen.

Orba, the second son of Partholon.

Oscar. 1. The son of Ossian, one of the Fianna.

2. Ossian had a second son, also called Oscar, by Niamh in Tir na nOg. Niamh named him after Ossian's other son of the same name and she named his brother Finn, after Ossian's father.

Ossian, the son of Finn and a poet, his mother Sadhbh had been transformed into ⟨ deer by a druid called 'the Dark Man'. Finn pursued the deer, who changed back into a woman, and she became his wife. When Finn was away the Dark Man took her away once more. Some time later, Finn, when out hunting, found a naked boy, who had been raised by a deer, presumably Ossian's mother. This was Ossian, his son. Ossian went to Tir na nOg with Niamh. Hundreds of years afterwards he rerurned to Ireland, still a youth. Owing to an accident, he toppled from his horse, from which he had been cautioned not to dismount, and he aged all the years which had taken no toll in Tir na nOg. He was then said to have met Saint Patrick.

Parthanan, an agricultural demon. His day is at the end of the harvest, when he will thresh all the corn left standing.

Partholon, a descendant of Magog, son of Japhet, he murdered his parents, hoping to seize power in his own country. Failing to do so, he fled to Ireland with his followers.

Partholonians, the people of Partholon who were eventually destroyed by a plague.

Phooka, a variant of the word 'pooka'.

Pig, there were once monstrous pigs now exterminated in Ireland. Their last stronghold was Imokilly, County Cork. A Geraldine killed that last boar of the race. Its body, rotting, caused an outbreak of disease so it was buried in a large chest.

Pine, after the death of Deirdre and Naoise, Conor had them buried at different sides of a lake to keep them apart; but a pine tree grew from each grave and they became intertwined.

Pishogue, a spell, coming from the Irish word *piseog*.

Plur na mBan, the name of the daughter of Ossian and Niamh, born to them during their sojourn together in Tir na nOg.

Polygamy, plural marriage of two sorts — polyandry (plurality of husbands) and polygyny (plurality of wives). The latter was permitted under the Irish pagan religion and enshrined in the Brehon Laws. The practice persisted even into Christian times.

Pooka, a solitary spirit or demon, which can assume various shapes — equine, aquiline, asinine, taurine or hircine. It was perhaps originally a deity. Wood-Martin suggests that stories of the pooka may represent a tradition of the woolly mammoth, which inhabited Ireland in prehistoric times.

Province, the Irish word for province, *cuige,* means 'a fifth'. There are four provinces in Ireland today and the question arises as to which was the fifth. A tradition, said to be as old as the ninth century, says it was Meath, a province made by the high king by taking territory from the other four. This seems strange, however, if the other four were already described as fifths and there is some question as to whether Munster, in fact, formed two provinces. The Rees brothers have argued in favour of the existence of an hierarchic symbolic function of each province as follows: Meath – kingship; Connacht – learning; Ulster – battle; Leinster – prosperity; Munster – music. Each province would be thus symbolically identified with the castle involved in each of these activities. The second Munster would have been the province of the aboriginal inhabitants of the island. P. O. Siochain has suggested that the fifth province was the lost land of Hy-Brasil. The Welsh Mabinogion gives an account of the origin of the five provinces of Ireland. After the island was devastated by Britons the sole survivors were five pregnant women and this resulted in the island's being divided into fifths.

Puck Fair, a festival held in the village of Killorglin in County Kerry. A buck goat (in Irish *poc,* pronounced 'puck'), white if possible and with decorated horns, is made king and driven around in triumph on the first day. On the third day he is released. The well-known song *An poc ar buile,* 'The Mad Goat', is associated with the festival, which, tradition has it, was imported into Killorglin from Kilgobnet. The festival was connected with Lughnasadh and dates at least from the seventeenth century. The whole business smacks of paganism and one thinks of rituals involving temporary kings and the Hebrew scapegoat, but the Kerry people tell the following legend about its origin. A young goatherd overheard Cromwellian soldiers plotting to destroy Killorglin. Not believed, he released the goats, led by the he-goat, into the soldiers' camp as they slept. As a result, the people of Killorglin have commemorated their hircine deliverer by holding the fair.

Raighne, a son of Finn.

Rath, a hapless wight who was lulled to sleep by mermaids, who tore him to pieces.

Red Branch, the body of knights who were the guardians of Ulster in the time of Cuchulain. In Irish they are called the *Craobh Rua.* The House of the Red Branch was where the sons of Usnach lodged with Deirdre after their return from Scotland.

Red Ridge, a member of the Fianna who once got irascible over the lack of pay and had to be quietened by Finn.

Reincarnation, *see* Metempsychosis.

Riata, the mythical ancestor of the Dal Riata, the tribe who, in the early Middle Ages, gave their name to the kingdom of Dalriada, which was partially in Antrim, partially in western Scotland.

Roc, a steward of Aengus, the love-god.

Ronan. 1. A king of Leinster. He was the father of Mael Fhothartaig. When the latter's mother died, Ronan married the daughter of Echaid, king of Dunseverick. She attempted to seduce his son and, having failed, accused him of adulterous desires towards her. Ronan had a warrior named Aedan slay his son, but, before he died of wounds (he was transfixed to his seat with a spear), he told Ronan the truth. Ronan was grief-stricken. There is a parallel between this tale and that of Theseus, Hippolytus and Phaedra. Ronan was an historical personage: he lived in the seventh century.

2. The saint who cursed Suibhne.

Ruadh and the three giantesses

Ron Cerr, a spy of Branduff, who entered the camp of Aedh, disguised as a leper with a wooden leg. He killed Aedh, pulling him from his horse and cutting off his head.

Ruadan, the son of Bres and Brigid who tried to slay Goibniu but was himself slain by the smith-god during the Second Battle of Moytura.

Ruadh, an Irish hero. When on a voyage his ship was stopped by three giantesses who took him to the seabed, where he slept with them. Saying they would bear his son, they made him promise to come back on the return voyage. He did not, so they pursued him with his son, but, seeing their pursuit would prove vain, they cut off the son's head and flung it after him.

Ruad Rofessa, the god of magic and druidism amongst the Tuatha De Danaan. He may have been identical with the Dagda.

Rudraide, a son of Partholon.

Sadhbh, the mother of Ossian.

Saidhthe Suaraighe. the bitch of evil, one of Cromm Dubh's dogs.

Salmon of Knowledge, red-spotted fish who acquired their knowledge by eating berries from a rowan tree in Ossory. The berries would fall from the tree into the well where the salmon were. Finegas caught one once and, delighted, left it cooking under the care of the young Finn mac Cool. Finn burned his thumb on the fish and licked that, so Finegas gave him the entire salmon and he thus gained the fish's knowledge.

Samaliliath, a Partholonian who introduced the drinking of ale to Ireland.

Samhain, a pagan festival which fell on 1 November, the onset of winter. It may have been the beginning of the Celtic new year. The barrows of the fairies were open at that time. The druids used to offer sacrifices and burn victims on Samhain Eve. Hallowe'en (Irish *Oiche Shamhna*) on 31 October is still a considerable festival in Ireland and Scotland and, indeed, in the United States, wither it has been exported. The festivities include the eating of a barmbrack (Irish *bairin breac* — speckled loaf) in which a ring is hidden. The finder of the ring, so the tradition runs, has a forthcoming marriage.

Samhair, a daughter of Finn who married Cormac Cas, king of Munster.

Scathach, a female warrior who was a tutor of the martial arts to Cuchulain.

Sceanb, the wife of Craiftine and the lover of Cormac Conloingeas.

Scenmend, the sister of Forgall. When Cuchulain carried Emer off, Scenmend pursued them and Cuchulain killed her in battle at a ford.

Sceolan, a hound of Finn, the brother of Bran. Finn's sister, Tuirean, was turned into a bitch by magic and gave birth to them.

Sciathbhreac, a member of the Fianna.

Scoriath, the king of Fir Morca and the father of Moriath. He helped Labraid, his son-in-law, re-establish himself as king of Leinster.

Scota. 1. The daughter of Pharoah Cincris, the wife of Niul and the mother of Gael.

2. The daughter of Pharoah Nectanebus who married Milesius. She fell fighting the Tuatha De Danaan. Her grave was in Kerry. These two persons, who figure in mediaeval Irish legend may have been the same person who became associated with different traditions. *Scotus* (fem. *Scota*) was the mediaeval Latin for an Irishman and Scota was an eponymous heroine of the Irish.

Scotland, this country (Irish *Alba*) figures in a number of Irish legends because of its contiguity with Ireland. In addition, the Highlanders and the Irish are basically of the same racial stock and share the Gaelic language and certain legendary traditions, notably those of the Fianna. In early mediaeval Latin the word *Scotus* signified an Irishman and Ireland was known as *Scotia Major* or simply *Scotia,* Scotland being known as *Scotia Minor.* The historical kingdom of Dalriada was partially in Ireland, partially in Scotland.

Seang, the daughter of the king of Scythia who married Milesius before he married Scota. She died before her husband left Scythia for Egypt.

Segda Saerlabraid, the son of the king and queen of Tir Tarraingthe who never came together except at his conception. We find here a note of asceticism of possible Christian origin in the legend.

Sencha, the chief judge and archpoet of Ulster in the days of Conor mac Nessa.

Sera, the father of Partholon.

Serpent, the serpent (Irish *nathair*) may have played a part in the religion of the pagan Irish and been associated with a horned god. A hint of this may be present in the story of Conall Cearnach and the serpent, where the serpent is seen, not as an adversary, but as the hero's companion. Serpents are not found in Ireland. Legend has it that Saint Patrick banished them, but their not being in Ireland was recorded before his time. It therefore seems strange that the serpent should figure in Irish religion, but it must be remembered that the Celts brought their religion with them from overseas. Patrick may have been credited with the banishment of the veneration of serpents. On the other hand there are traditions of lacustrine monsters in Ireland — perhaps it was they which were venerated. In early writings the distinction between a serpent and a dragon was often blurred or non-existent. There is some evidence that the Irish had a conception of a world serpent like the Norse Midgard serpent.

Setanta, the real name of Cuchulain. There may be some connection with the British tribe of the Setantii who inhabited the north-west of England.

Seth, a biblical character, son of Adam and Eve. In Irish legend he and three daughters of Cain were the first people to see Ireland.

Shannon City, according to legend, is a city lying under the Shannon. It appears once every seven years. Whoever sees it will die.

Sid, a fairy mound.

Simeon Breac, the son of Starn. After the Nemedian defeat by the Fomorians, he and his followers went to Thrace where the people were enslaved and became the ancestors of the Firbolg.

Simon Magus, the New Testament personage. According to Irish legend, his sons raped Tlachtga.

Sineach, the monster, also called 'the muirdris', slain by Fergus mac Leide.

Sionan, a woman who caught one of the Salmon of Knowledge which were supposed to be off limits to her sex. However, when she began to eat it, water shot up and carried her off to that river, the Shannon, which now bears her name. Perhaps we have here an euhemerised river goddess.

Slangia, a son of Partholon.

Smirgat, a wife of Finn who warned him that, if he ever drank from a horn, his death would follow.

Sovranty of Ireland, the abstract Sovranty of Ireland is personified as a woman or goddess in a number of tales.

Sowlth, a bright supernatural creature without shape.

Spain, this country figures in Irish legend and is a substitution for overseas realms to which a vague designation was originally applied. It may sometimes have been substituted in the Middle Ages for the Celtic otherworld.

Sparan Scillinge, literally 'shilling purse'. A fairy purse, inexhaustible, which a leprechaun will give you, if you can hold him spellbound with your gaze.

Sreng, alternative form of Seang.

Starn, a son of Nemed.

Stoat, an animal, *Mustela erminea,* in Ireland wrongly called a weasel. These animals are believed to be witches, shrivelled up. A purse made from the skin of one of them will never be empty.

Suibhne, a king who, according to legend, was compelled by the curse of Saint Ronan to assume the characteristics of a bird, such a frequenting the branches of trees, while retaining the form of a man.

Sun Worship, heliolatry or sun worship would appear to have been known amongst the pagan Irish. On Mount Callan, near Ennis, is the location of an altar of the sun, where there used to be festivals annually on May Day and Midsummer Eve. The Irish continued to hold the Midsummer Eve festival until about 1895. A standing stone near Macroon is called 'the Stone of the Sun'. According to Keating an early Irish heliolater was MacGreine, who adopted this name, meaning 'son of the sun', because of his religious propensities. The dolmens called 'Beds of Dermot and Grania', which Keating assures his readers were not such at all, originally have been sun monuments, the connection with the Fenian elopement being due to a confusion between the name 'Grania' (Irish *Grainne,* perhaps from *gra,* love) and *grian,* genetive *greine,* meaning 'sun'. The

A sparan scillinge, an inexhaustible fairy purse, was the reward for being able to hold a leprechaun spellbound with your gaze

reader's attention is also drawn to the fairy queen Grian whose name means 'sun'; perhaps she was originally a sun goddess. It is also drawn to Gille Greine, whose mother was a sunbeam.

Tadhg, an important druid who opposed Cumhal's marriage to his daughter Murna for he had supernatural knowledge to the effect that, if this wedding occurred, he would lose his ancestral seat. Cumhal abducted Murna so Tadhg persuaded King Conn to send troops after him. The battle resulting in Cumhal's death ensued.

Tailtiu, a Firbolg, she married one of the Tuatha De Danaan and was the foster-mother of Lugh. She cleared the Forest of Breg, making it into a plain. As a result, she died. Lugh decreed a feast in her honour.

Tara, a hill in central Ireland, originally a place of sepulture. A passage grave dating from about 2100 B.C. has been found there. It became in time a place of royal residence. According to mediaeval writers, it was the seat of the high kingship in early times. However, the high kingship does not seem to have been a political reality until the ninth century. The Ui Neill dynasty, who became high kings and had originally been kings of Tara, retained this title even after their removal elsewhere. F. J. Byrne argues that their reason for clinging tenaciously to the title was that it has possessed a cultic significance — perhaps even a cultic significance for the entire island. The concept of kingship amongst the pagan Irish may well have embodied a sacerdotal function. Tara itself may have been looked on as a bastion against the forces of the otherworld.

Tabhfheis, a ceremony used in the choosing of a king. A man would eat the flesh of a bull and be put to sleep by magic. The man of whom he dreamed would become king.

Tea, an Irish goddess, the patroness of Tara.

Teideach, and his brother Clonnach, were, in oral legend, sons of Cromm Dubh, who is depicted, not as an idol, but as a chief overcome by Saint Patrick.

Tethra, a Fomorian; perhaps originally an early Irish sea god.

Three Gods of Craftmanship, these were Credne, Goibniu and Luchtar.

Three-Headed Bird, a creature that devestated Ireland until slain by Amairgene.

Tigernmas, a king of Ireland who, according to the *Annals of the Four Masters,* reigned from *Anno Mundi* 3580 to 3656. His name signifies 'lord of death'. He fought against the Milesians. With his people he prostrated himself before Cromm Cruach. They did this so frequently and with such frenzy that many injured themselves and died.

Tiobraide Tireach, a legendary king of Ulster who slew Conn of the Hundred Battles as he was making ready to celebrate the feis at Tara.

Tir fo Thuinn, the land under wave, a legendary country.

Tir na mBan, the country of the women whither Bran was summoned by its queen and where they stayed many years, thinking they had remained there but a single year.

Tir na mBeo, the country of the living, a legendary land. The daughter of its king was kidnapped by a giant but Ossian, on his way to Tir na nOg, slew the abductor.

Tir na nOg, the land of youth, corresponding to the Eilean na hOige of Scottish tradition. In this country, one was supposed to stay young eternally. It was situated somewhere in the Atlantic. Its most famous visitor was Ossian. The idea that there were islands such as Tir na nOg in the Atlantic may have arisen from cloud formations appearing to be solid land. It may also have sprung up because artifacts from America were sometimes washed up in Ireland, having been carried by the Gulf Stream, yielding a clue that there were human populations in or beyond the Atlantic.

Tir Tairngiri, the Land of Promise, the territory ruled by Manannan.

Tiachtga, an Irish goddess who, at one fatal birth, produced three sons, each by a different father.

Todga, a slave of Dealgnaid who had an adulterous affair with her.

Toice Bhrean, the guardian of the well from which Lough Gur came.

Tory Island, an island off the north coast of Ireland, in County Donegal. It was said to have been the headquarters of the Fomorians. Conaing had his tower there, which was captured by the Nemedians.

Treasure, hidden treasure is usually protected by spirits who frighten off searchers by assuming hideous shapes. Water monsters and black cats are supposed to guard treasures.

Treasure Bag of the Fianna, made of the skin of Aoife, this contained a number of treasures such a Manannan's knife and shirt. These treasures would be in the bag at full tide but would vanish at ebb-tide.

Tuan Mac Carell, a Partholonian who survived the plague which destroyed that race. One morning he found himself transformed into a stag and became sovereign of the stags of Ireland. Growing old he was transformed into a wild boar. Then he was transformed into an eagle. After this, he was metamorphosed into a salmon. This hapless fish was caught and eaten by the wife of Cavell who then gave birth to Tuan as a child.

Tuatha De Danaan, according to legend, the race which inhabited Ireland before the coming of the Milesians. It is agreed by mythologists that they were, in fact, the gods of the pagan Irish, who had been demoted to heroes by the Christians. They came from a northern country, where they had four cities — Falias, Gorias, Finias and Murias. In Ireland they fought first the Firbolg and then the Fomorians. Their king when they arrived was Nuada. They ruled Ireland for an unknown length of time and were then defeated by the Milesians.

Tuathal Techtmar, a legendary king of Ireland, the father of Fithir and Dairine.

Tuirbe, the father of Goibniu and a great axe thrower.

Tuirean, Finn's sister, who was enchanted and turned into a bitch, in which state she gave birth to Finn's hounds, Bran and Sceolan. According to another version, she was Finn's sister-in-law. Her husband, Illan, had a fairy mistress who, in jealousy, transformed Tuirean. When Illan promised to abandon Tuirean the fairy turned her back into a human.

Tuireann, Sons of, these were Brian, Iuchar and Iucharba, who slew Cian, father of Lugh and, in retaliation, were ordered by Lugh to obtain for him the following articles: (1) the three apples from the Orient Garden; (2) the healing swineskin of King Tuis of Greece; (3) the Luin, a spear of King Pisar of Persia; (4) the chariot and horses of King Dobar of Siogair; (5) the magic pigs of King Easal of the Golden Pillars; (6) Fail-Inis, the whelp of the king of Ioruaidh; and (7) a cooking spit of the women of Fairhead Island. In addition, they had to shout three times on the hill of Miochaoin. They were successful, but died as a result of their endeavours.

Tuan MacCarell was metamorphosed into a salmon and eaten by the wife of Cavell

Uacthach, the daughter of Scathach, she became enamoured of Cuchulain.

Uaitne, the harp of the Dagda, which was captured by the Fomorians. The Dagda had put an enchantment on it to prevent it sounding until he called it. He traced it to a feasting house and summoned it. Uaitne sprang from the wall on which it was placed and went to him, killing nine men in the process.

Ugaine Mor, an ancient legendary king of Ireland.

Ui Corra, the heroes of one of the *immrama* (voyages); in fact, a mediaeval composition for purposes of moral edification which tells how the three Ui Corra — Lochan, Emne and Silvester — go on voyages and land on various islands.

Uigreann, a victim of Finn's prowess. It was said the sons of Uigreann killed Finn or assisted a grandson of Goll to do so.

Usnach, the sons of Usnach were Naoise, Ardan and Ainnle.

Vainche, a son of Finn.

Victor, according to tradition, was an angel attached to Saint Patrick, who met him on the road and told him to return to a barn he had quitted, for he was to die there. In origin his name may be connected with Victoricus, in Saint Patrick's dream.

Voyages, (*immrama*) involving wonders were an important feature of Irish legend. The voyage of Bran is set in pagan times; those of the Ui Corra, Maeldun and Saint Brendan in Christian times. It has been suggested that some of these journeys may have been connected with belief in immortality.

Vulcan, the Roman smith god, also called Mulciber, equated to the Greek Hephaestus. According to Irish legend, it was from him the Morrigan and her comrades obtained the spear that was to kill Cuchulain.

Water-Horse, Irish *each uisce,* a term applied to lake monsters.

Water Sherie, a supernatural creature, something in the nature of an *ignis fatuua* or Will-o'-the-wisp.

Weasel, an animal, *mustela nivalis,* not found in Ireland. However, in Ireland the term 'weasel' is incorrectly applied to the stoat, *mustela erminea,* and Irish folk belief regarding the weasel, in fact, applies to the stoat.

Whitethorn, this plant was said to be unlucky.

Willow, this tree was supposed to give one an uncontrollable urge to dance.

Witch-Hare, a hare which is in reality a witch who has transformed herself. Witch-hares were said to steal milk from cattle.

Witch of Bolus, a sister of the Witch of Dingle and the Cailleach Beara.

Witch of Dingle, a sister of the Cailleach Beara who was said to have lived to more than three hundred years of age. She always covered the top of her head, never let the soles of her feet touch the ground and never slept unless sleepy.

Wren, a bird called in Irish *dreolin,* much despised by the Irish for wrens perched on Irish drums when Irish soldiers were about to attack the Cromwellians. Such was the noise they made, says the legend, that the Cromwellians were roused, fell upon the Irish and slaughtered them. On Saint Stephen's Day (December 26th), sometimes called 'Boxing Day', bands of wren boys hunt the wren in retaliation for its betrayal of the Irish. An Irish folktale says that the wren became the king of the birds by flying higher than any other. It achieved this by perching on an eagle and, when the eagle had flown as high as it could, the wren flew a little higher.

bibliography

Arbois de Jubainville, H., *The Irish Mythological Cycle and Celtic Mythology* (Dublin, 1903).

Ashe, G., *Land to the West* (London, 1962).

Benwell, G. and Waugh, A., *Sea Enchantress* (London, 1961).

Blacam, A. de, *Gaelic Literature Surveyed* (Dublin, 1933).

Byrne, F. J., *Irish Kings and High-Kings* (London, 1973).

Byrne, P. F., *Witchcraft in Ireland* (Cork, 1967).

Campbell, J. J., *Legends of Ireland* (London, 1955).

Colum, P., *The Voyagers* (New York, 1925).

Croker, T. C. and Clifford, S., *Legends of Kerry* (Tralee, 1975).

Dillon, M., *The Cycles of the Kings* (London, 1946).

Dillon, M. and Chadwick, N. K., *The Celtic Realms* (London, 1972).

Filip, J., *Celtic Civilization and its Heritage* (Wellingborough, 1977).

Gray, L. H., *The Mythology of all Races* (New York, 1964).

Gregory, A., *Cuchulain of Muirthemhne* (London, 1902).

Gregory, A., *Gods and Fighting Men* (London, 1904).

Harley, T., *Moon Lore* (Rutland, Vt., 1970).

Hartland, E. S., *The Science of Fairy Tales* (London, 1891).

Herm, G., *The Celts* (London, 1976).

Hull, E., *Folklore of the British Isles* (London, 1928).

Hyde, D., *Legends of Saints and Sinners* (London, n.d.).

Joyce, P. W., *Irish Names of Places* (Dublin, n.d.).

Kavanagh, P., *Irish Mythology: a Dictionary* (New York, 1958-59).

Keating, G., *The History of Ireland* (New York, 1857).

Leach, M. (ed.), *Funk and Wagnalls Standard Dictionary of Folklore, Mythology and Legend* (New York, 1949-50).

MacCana, P., *Celtic Mythology* (London, 1970).

McGarry, M. (ed.), *Great Fairy Tales of Ireland* (London, 1973).

Mahon, M. P., *Ireland's Fairy Lore* (Boston, 1919).

O'Connor, D., *St Patrick's Purgatory, Lough Derg* (Dublin, 1895).

O'Farrell, P., *Superstitions of the Irish Country People* (Dublin, 1978).

O'Rahilly, T. F., *Early Irish History and Mythology* (Dublin, 1946).

O Siochain, P. A., *Aran: Islands of Legend* (Dublin, 1962).

Parsons, E. B., *Tales of Tara* (Dublin, 1933).

Piggott, S., *The Druids* (London, 1968).

Rees, A. and Rees, B., *Celtic Heritage* (London, 1961).

Rolleston, T. W., *Myths and Legends of the Celtic Race* (London, 1912).

Seymour, St. J. D., *Irish Witchcraft and Demonology* (Dublin, 1913).

Seymour, St. J. D., *St Patrick's Purgatory* (Dundalk, n.d.).

Sjoestedt, M. L., *Gods and Heroes of the Celts* (London, 1949).

Spaan, D. B., *The Otherworld in Early Irish Literature* (Ann Arbor, 1978).

Spence, L., *A Dictionary of Medieval Romance and Romance Writers* (London, 1913).

Ua Cleirigh, A., *The History of Ireland to the Coming of Henry II* (Port Washington, 1970).

Wentz, W. Y. E., *The Fairy Faith in Celtic Countries* (London, 1911).

White, C., *A History of Irish Fairies* (Dublin, 1976).

Wilde, J. F., *Ancient Legends, Mystic Charms and Superstitions of Ireland* (London, 1888).

Wilde, W. R., *Irish Popular Superstitions* (Dublin, 1852).

Wood-Martin, W. G., *Traces of the Elder Faiths in Ireland* (London, 1902).

Yeats, W. B., *Fairy and Folk Tales of Ireland* (Gerrards Cross, 1977).